FBML Essentials

Other resources from O'Reilly

Related titles

Facebook Cookbook™
CSS: The Definitive Guide
Programming Collective Intelligence
Facebook: The Missing Manual
JavaScript: The Definitive Guide

oreilly.com

oreilly.com is more than a complete catalog of O'Reilly books. You'll also find links to news, events, articles, weblogs, sample chapters, and code examples.

oreillynet.com is the essential portal for developers interested in open and emerging technologies, including new platforms, programming languages, and operating systems.

Conferences

O'Reilly Media brings diverse innovators together to nurture the ideas that spark revolutionary industries. We specialize in documenting the latest tools and systems, translating the innovator's knowledge into useful skills for those in the trenches. Visit *conferences.oreilly.com* for our upcoming events.

Safari Bookshelf (*safari.oreilly.com*) is the premier online reference library for programmers and IT professionals. Conduct searches across more than 1,000 books. Subscribers can zero in on answers to time-critical questions in a matter of seconds. Read the books on your Bookshelf from cover to cover or simply flip to the page you need. Try it today for free.

FBML Essentials

Jesse Stay

O'REILLY®

Beijing • Cambridge • Farnham • Köln • Sebastopol • Taipei • Tokyo

FBML Essentials
by Jesse Stay

Copyright © 2008 Stay N' Alive Productions, LLC. All rights reserved.
Printed in the United States of America.

Published by O'Reilly Media, Inc., 1005 Gravenstein Highway North, Sebastopol, CA 95472.

O'Reilly books may be purchased for educational, business, or sales promotional use. Online editions are also available for most titles (*http://safari.oreilly.com*). For more information, contact our corporate/institutional sales department: 800-998-9938 or *corporate@oreilly.com*.

Editor: Mary E. Treseler
Production Editor: Sarah Schneider
Copyeditor: Sarah Schneider
Proofreader: Sada Preisch
Indexer: Fred Brown
Cover Designer: Karen Montgomery
Interior Designer: David Futato
Illustrator: Robert Romano

Printing History:
July 2008: First Edition.

Nutshell Handbook, the Nutshell Handbook logo, and the O'Reilly logo are registered trademarks of O'Reilly Media, Inc. *FBML Essentials*, the image of a white-throated dipper, and related trade dress are trademarks of O'Reilly Media, Inc.

Many of the designations used by manufacturers and sellers to distinguish their products are claimed as trademarks. Where those designations appear in this book, and O'Reilly Media, Inc. was aware of a trademark claim, the designations have been printed in caps or initial caps.

While every precaution has been taken in the preparation of this book, the publisher and author assume no responsibility for errors or omissions, or for damages resulting from the use of the information contained herein.

ISBN: 978-0-596-51918-6

[M]

1215790051

Table of Contents

Foreword

When it initially launched, the Internet transformed the way humans connected. Soon enough we had access to unlimited content at our fingertips. Within a matter of years, people were changing the way they communicated, and by the late 1990s, social networks were beginning to make their transformative impact. You could say a lot of things about the future of social networks, but one thing you can't disagree with is that Facebook was a catalyst for a substantial redevelopment and redesign of the way that we share information about ourselves on the Web.

For developers, the launch of the Facebook Platform in 2007 brought about many things: a new language to learn, an easy way to build valuable user relationships and access personal data, and most importantly, the opportunity to easily and quickly launch an application that can potentially reach millions of people. Although the initial opportunity for application developers was monumental, the opportunity that exists today should not be discounted. Today, developers can build applications that reach a large portion of users on Facebook, the fifth largest website on the Internet.

Not only can your applications have massive reach, but there is also a substantial business opportunity to develop applications for others who recognize the opportunity. Whether you are an entrepreneurial developer or you are simply in pursuit of knowledge, you will not be disappointed with what Facebook has to offer. As somebody who is a self-taught developer, I launched my first application within 45 minutes and reached over 40,000 users. I experienced firsthand the opportunity that the platform presents. Although Facebook does have the occasional hiccup, you will not find any other platform like it.

Whether you are programming in PHP, .NET, Ruby on Rails, or any other language, you will surely be satisfied with the Facebook Platform. But keep in mind that although it is easy to develop and launch an application quickly, maintaining your application takes time. Once a week, Facebook administrators fix the platform bugs that can occasionally make your application go down. Your app won't be destroyed, but these disruptions are a part of life while developing on Facebook. You are at the forefront of development and this is just part of what it's like to be on the bleeding edge.

If I could give you one word of advice for success on Facebook, it would be this: community. Leverage the developer community for all it's worth because this is one of the most active developer communities I have ever seen. People will constantly give you feedback, and they also will alert you to errors and to other developers' bad practices. The Facebook Platform is by no means a typical platform. It is constantly evolving and will continuously be under development. Use this book as a way to build a solid base, and make sure that you keep up-to-date with all the changes taking place on the platform.

Finally, good luck on your path to building the next big thing on Facebook. It is a challenging task, but for anyone who is passionate about an idea, anything can be accomplished.

—Nick O'Neill
AllFacebook.com

Preface

The Facebook Platform Emerges

On May 24, 2007, the world changed forever when Facebook CEO Mark Zuckerberg announced that Facebook was opening its platform, or "social graph," to developers (see *http://www.facebook.com/press/releases.php?p=3102*). This update would allow developers to access a wealth of information, from names and birth dates to friend information and the ways that users link together. Never since the invention of the web browser has an API made such an impact on the world. For many, Facebook has become the web browser for the social Internet.

Since Zuckerberg's announcement at the F8 conference, software developers around the world—including myself—have rushed to be the first to make their millions in a literal gold rush not seen since the dot-com boom. In a matter of days, we have watched our applications go from zero to millions of users.

The Facebook Platform has opened up a wealth of knowledge to us as developers. The API gives developers the flexibility through PHP, Java, Perl, Ruby, .NET, and virtually any other language to access user information through a simple REST interface. A data access language called Facebook Query Language (FQL) allows simple SQL-like statements to retrieve information through that API. The Facebook Data Store API gives developers a location in which to store their regularly accessed data. A JavaScript™ client library allows client-side access to the API, requiring only simple HTML to render data from Facebook. On top of all that, Facebook released the Facebook Markup Language (FBML), which lets you render data on a page without the need to always access the API.

Each one of these aspects of the Facebook Platform could warrant its own book. *FBML Essentials* is intended to be your guide to perhaps the most important and basic component of the platform, FBML.

FBML

The Facebook Markup Language can be compared to the "icing" on the cake that is the Facebook API. Although FBML is not completely necessary for writing a successful Facebook application, it brings to the table many features that make development on Facebook more efficient, and in the end, it makes life as a social applications developer much better. For instance, you may have previously retrieved the name of the user of your application through a simple `users.getLoggedInUser` API call on the server. But perhaps you've discovered that it's not worth going through the entire process of authenticating the user on the server side and returning the application user's name. Or, what if you want to further separate your presentation logic from your application logic? A name, after all, is not necessarily something that should be calculated or processed. You may want to have your HTML in a file that's entirely separate from the files you are making API calls from, and therefore something as simple as a name might make sense to include with your HTML.

For these reasons, FBML can be an ideal tool for organizing your Facebook applications and, most of all, for reducing the amount of API requests you have to make to Facebook. One FBML tag on a page takes no HTTP requests off your servers in order to render, whereas a simple API call for the same information could take one HTTP request to authenticate with Facebook and another to retrieve the information desired. This additional overhead slows down your application, and in an environment where you could easily have millions of users using your app, you want to save every request you can.

FBML is a tool, a resource, for you as a developer to make your work in the Facebook API more efficient. FBML brings a lot of power to developers, allowing them to use API calls only when most needed. As I will show in the "Hello World" example in Chapter 1, an entire simple application can be created using FBML alone!

The intent of this book is to get you to the point where you, as a Facebook developer, can decide when FBML makes sense for your application and when you are better off using the Facebook API. It's my hope that you can continue to use this book as a resource as your development skills mature.

One topic not covered in this book is the Social Network Markup Language (SNML) and the social networking website Bebo (*http://www.bebo.com*). SNML is a tag language extremely similar to FBML that works on the recently launched Bebo Developers Platform. However, Bebo also supports certain FBML tags, so this book should serve as a reference for developing on Bebo as well as on Facebook. I will update this book's Facebook Page (*http://page.fbmlessentials.com*) with more information regarding Bebo's SNML and supported FBML tags as this new platform progresses.

Keep in mind that the only FBML tags that Bebo does not yet support are `<fb:mobile/>`, `<fb:visible-to-connection/>`, `<fb:attachment-preview/>`, and `<fb:is-in-network/>`. Therefore, use this book as you see fit for your Bebo application development! You can read a great how-to article on porting apps from Facebook to Bebo (written by Blake Commagere, developer of the Zombies, Vampires, and Werewolves games on Facebook) here: *http://dev.aol.com/article/2008/porting-your-facebook-app-to-bebo*.

Developer Guidelines

Before we get started, we should go over some guidelines. Although there are no "official" guidelines for development at the time of this writing, other than the Facebook Developer Terms of Service (*http://developers.facebook.com/terms.php*), there are some unwritten rules generally accepted by the Facebook developer community. Some of these may not make sense for you until we get further on in the book, so you may want to bookmark this section for later reference. Taken from the Facebook Developer Wiki, the following rules were written up by a few developers outside of the Facebook organization (see *http://wiki.developers.facebook.com/index.php/Developer_Guidelines_Manual*):

Invites

- Do not force a user to send invites.
  - Show the invite page *after* performing an action.
  - Make it clear the action has been performed, and that the user is not forced to send invites to continue using the app/perform the action.
  - You may also include a link to the invite page somewhere in your application.
  - Sending invites for an app using another app is prohibited by the Terms of Service (TOS).

- — Do not include users who already have the app installed in the friend selector (or variants).

- Do not use invites for ranking purposes.
  - — When using invites as part of an application's function, such as user ranking, make sure there are other ranking methods that can replace invites.
  - — Using invites alone increases the chances for the application, and the user's rank within it, to lose value.
- Do not use blocked markup, or attempt to use sketchy methods to gain a user's attention in the Requests page.
  - — Usage of CSS, large fonts, and other prohibited markup is looked down upon by the community. We highly discourage this.
  - — Usage of blocked markup can also lead to the removal of your application.

Notifications/News Feed

- Do not post *every* action your app makes.
  - — Simply send/post when the *primary function* of an app is performed.
  - — Too many notifications and/or News Feed stories increase the chance of an app being blocked and/or being viewed as a spammy app by users.

User Interface

- Do not require *install* or *login* in the main canvas page.
  - — Doing so increases the chances of the *user not using your application*, or just installing it and not using it.
  - — We recommend you have a page that entices the user to use the app, but *do not mislead* the user with false data.
  - — Show what your application does, not a simple "Add this app and you'll see what this is about" or misleading descriptions.
- *Do not require both* an install and a login.
  - — Doing so is pointless. Only use one, as deemed necessary.
  - — It is a *nuisance* to users, and probably lowers chances of actual app usage.
- Do not use JavaScript alerts.
  - — JavaScript alerts are *annoying* to the user, disrupt the smoothness of the experience, and do not fit in well with the Facebook user interface.

Naming

- Do not use the *same or similar name* as an existing app without expressed permission of original author(s).
  - —Using similar names confuses users.
  - —It may be a copyright violation, when applicable.

In addition to the preceding guidelines, it is my opinion that you should conform to the following rules as well:

- Keep your applications in a format compatible with Facebook.
  - —Your application should feel like it is part of Facebook, with the same look, colors, and formatting.
- Use FBML wherever possible to replace API calls.
  - —This reduces overall overhead and shortens development time.
  - —This also gives you a few more features, such as invite forms (covered later in this book), which aren't accessible via the API.
- Where FBML is not possible, render the page as FBML and use an `<fb:iframe/>` tag for the areas that need to be rendered outside of FBML.
- Separate your presentation from your application logic!
  - —This can be a huge timesaver for you in the future, and it gives you a single location in which to store your FBML tags without mixing them up in your code.

Useful Resources

As a Facebook developer, like any master of a trade, you cannot succeed without the proper tools and resources. There are a few websites you'll need to become familiar with if you are going to stay up-to-date in your skills. I'll list these here.

Tools and Documentation

Facebook developers website (http://developers.facebook.com)
: The official Facebook site for developers and developer documentation.

Facebook Developer Wiki (http://wiki.developers.facebook.com)
: The official Facebook wiki for developers. Go here for the most up-to-date documentation on any FBML, FBJS, or development-related information. Since it's a wiki, it allows anyone to update the content, and it is updated quite frequently.

Facebook FBML Test Console (http://developers.facebook.com/tools.php?fbml)
: A console to test out your FBML. You enter the FBML in the box provided, and it outputs the rendered markup as HTML.

Facebook Developers Forum (http://forum.developers.facebook.com/)
: Want to ask other Facebook developers a question? This is the place to do so, and to share issues and interact with the Facebook development team.

Facebook bug tracking and submission (http://bugs.developers.facebook.com/)
: If you find bugs in FBML or in any of your Facebook development, submit them here. Search for an existing bug and see its status, or submit a new bug.

The FBML Essentials Facebook app (http://apps.facebook.com/fbmlessentials)
: The official Facebook app for *FBML Essentials*. I'm creating this app as I write this book, and I will keep the app up-to-date as the platform evolves. Here you can see working examples of the most-used FBML tags on Facebook, take trivia quizzes, and challenge your friends on their FBML knowledge! Become a fan of the app for updates as it evolves.

The FBML Essentials Facebook Page (http://page.fbmlessentials.com)
: The official Facebook Page for *FBML Essentials*. Here I'll post updates to this book, news, photos, videos, fan pictures, and more. Visit this Page to discuss the book and FBML development.

News and Information About Facebook Development

Stay N' Alive blog, by Jesse Stay (http://staynalive.com)
: "Stay" up-to-date with the latest and greatest in Facebook and social development news and other topics. This is my blog, a must-read if you are a reader of this book.

Jesse's FriendFeed stream (http://friendfeed.com/jessestay)
: Want to follow what I'm doing, what I'm interested in, and what I'm linking to? Follow my FriendFeed stream and see what I'm talking about, get in on the conversation, and find out where I am on Twitter, my blogs, and more.

The Social Coding FriendFeed stream (http://friendfeed.com/rooms/social-coding)
: This is a great place I have set up for discussing and learning about developing for social websites and social networks in general.

FacebookAdvice blog (http://facebookadvice.com)
: The official blog for my previous book, *I'm On Facebook—Now What???* (Happy About). It covers how-tos, advice, tips, and tricks related to Facebook in general.

Facebook blog (http://blog.facebook.com)
: The official Facebook blog, targeted to a nondeveloper audience.

Facebook Platform status feed (http://www.facebook.com/developers/message.php)
: Subscribe to this feed in your RSS reader if you want to be notified whenever the platform goes down, whenever updates are made to the platform, or whenever there is an update that could affect your code.

Facebook developer news (http://developers.facebook.com/news.php?blog=1)
: The official Facebook developers blog. Subscribe to this feed for all the latest developer news, straight from Facebook. News will usually be here before any other source.

Facebook developers marketplace (http://www.facebook.com/developers/marketplace)
: Looking for a job that needs a Facebook developer? This is the place to look, and it's also the place to post jobs related to Facebook development.

AllFacebook, by Nick O'Neill (http://allfacebook.com)
: Facebook news and reviews, by the folks at SocialTimes.com.

FaceReviews, by Rodney Rumford (http://facereviews.com)
: Facebook apps reviews, news, and other info, by Rodney Rumford.

InsideFacebook, by Justin Smith (http://insidefacebook.com)
: More Facebook news and reviews, by Justin Smith.

Is This Book For You?

To understand the principles in this book, you need to at least know the principles of HTML design and development, CSS principles, and some JavaScript. FBML is a tag language, based on a pseudo-XML format, just like HTML. Therefore, having a background in HTML will help you understand the concepts taught in this book. This book is intended for the experienced developer who wants to get started in the new world of Facebook development, and it will serve as an introduction to the FBML tag language for the Facebook API. You can also refer to this book throughout your Facebook development efforts whenever you need it.

In Chapter 1, I will brief you on the basics of setting up a very simple Facebook application. It has been my experience that although many Facebook developers have been working on apps since the platform launched, many of us still do not fully understand the details of what is involved in setting up an application. If you already know all that, you may want to skip ahead to Chapter 2, but in the end it may be a good refresher for you to go through the "Hello World" process with me.

Some Terms You Should Know

To fully understand what I am talking about in this book, there are a few terms you should be familiar with before you start reading. I'll list these here:

Facebook Platform
: The *Facebook Platform* is the underlying engine that powers the Facebook API. It is what parses your FBML and enables you as a developer to write apps on top of Facebook.

F8
: *F8* is the developers conference that first made the Facebook Platform popular. At this conference in 2007, Mark Zuckerberg, founder of Facebook, announced the launch of the Facebook Platform for all developers. At the time of this writing, another F8 conference is scheduled for July 2008.

Facebook profile
: Each user on Facebook has a *profile* that displays information about who they are, what their interests are, their birthday, location, and other information. At the time of this writing, the profile is a single page within Facebook. In July 2008 a new design will be launched, which will spread the user's profile across multiple pages via tabs.

Facebook Page
: When I mention a *Facebook Page* with a capital "P," I am referring to what is the equivalent of a Facebook profile for a business or company. Each Facebook Page provides a place for the business to put a description of itself, an image, and other miscellaneous information. Each Page also has a place for a discussion board, a Wall, images, and videos. The Facebook Page even allows apps to be installed that can be customized for businesses instead of just single users.

Facebook application (or app)
: The *Facebook app* is the core of what we are building in this book. It has many different integration points for engaging the user and for informing the user's friends about how they use your app. By the time you finish this

book, you should be able to create a very basic Facebook application. I strongly suggest you research the Facebook API and see what else you can do with your app.

Canvas page
: The *canvas page* is essentially any page within your application that is not a profile box. Clicking on the link of any application in Facebook will take you to its canvas page. As a developer, you are in full control of your canvas page. You can advertise on canvas pages and monetize them however you want, and you earn 100% of the revenues!

> At the time of this writing, the only parts of Facebook you can edit are the profile and the canvas page. The new design will introduce another part you can edit—a customizable "tab page"—but we won't go into detail about that here because Facebook has not released much information at this time. Stay tuned to this book's Facebook Page at *http://page.fbmlessentials.com* to be kept up-to-date on that feature.

Profile box
: At the time of this writing, each Facebook profile allows you to install applications on your profile page, which is just a single page on Facebook. When the new tabbed profile design is rolled out in July, you will be able to add *profile boxes* via a simple click on a button created with the `<fb:add-section-button/>` tag (see that tag's description in Chapter 3). You can use this button to specify where within your profile you'd like to add an application. You can set an app to appear on a special "Boxes" tab on your profile, or as additional information on the "Info" tab, or as a narrow box on other tabs.

New design
: Slated for release in July 2008, the new Facebook design will center around the user profile. This profile will be split into tabs to encourage more interaction between users and—most importantly for readers of this book—to provide more integration points for app developers. Facebook Pages should be unaffected by the new profile design, and almost all FBML tags covered in this book will still be applicable. I have tried to remove or note those that will be deprecated by the time this book goes to print.

Although the tags listed in this book will continue to work within Facebook's new design, keep in mind that your integration points will change. I have done my best to note where that may be the case, but at the time of this writing, the release notes are too vague to fully predict everything you will need to know. For this reason, please check back often to this book's Facebook Page at *http://page.fbmlessentials.com*, and I will post updates there.

Conventions Used in This Book

The following typographical conventions are used in this book:

Italic
: Indicates new terms, URLs, email addresses, filenames, and file extensions.

`Constant width`
: Used for program listings as well as within paragraphs to refer to program elements such as variable or function names, databases, data types, environment variables, statements, and keywords.

`Constant width bold`
: Shows commands or other text that should be typed literally by the user.

`Constant width italic`
: Shows text that should be replaced with user-supplied values or by values determined by context.

This icon signifies a tip, suggestion, or general note.

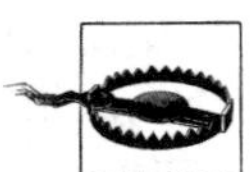

This icon indicates a warning or caution.

Using Code Examples

This book is here to help you get your job done. In general, you may use the code in this book in your programs and documentation. You do not need to contact us for permission unless you're reproducing a significant portion of the code. For example, writing a program that uses several chunks of code from this book does not require permission. Selling or distributing a CD-ROM of examples from O'Reilly books does require permission. Answering a question by citing this book and quoting example code does not require permission. Incorporating a significant amount of example code from this book into your product's documentation does require permission.

We appreciate, but do not require, attribution. An attribution usually includes the title, author, publisher, and ISBN. For example: "*FBML Essentials* by Jesse Stay. Copyright 2008 Stay N' Alive Productions, LLC, 978-0-596-51918-6."

If you feel your use of code examples falls outside fair use or the permission given above, feel free to contact us at *permissions@oreilly.com*.

How to Contact Us

Please address comments and questions concerning this book to the publisher:

O'Reilly Media, Inc.
1005 Gravenstein Highway North
Sebastopol, CA 95472
800-998-9938 (in the United States or Canada)
707-829-0515 (international or local)
707-829-0104 (fax)

We have a web page for this book, where we list errata, examples, and any additional information. You can access this page at:

http://www.oreilly.com/catalog/9780596519186

To comment or ask technical questions about this book, send email to:

bookquestions@oreilly.com

For more information about our books, conferences, Resource Centers, and the O'Reilly Network, see our website at:

http://www.oreilly.com

Safari® Books Online

Safari Books Online

When you see a Safari® Books Online icon on the cover of your favorite technology book, that means the book is available online through the O'Reilly Network Safari Bookshelf.

Safari offers a solution that's better than e-books. It's a virtual library that lets you easily search thousands of top tech books, cut and paste code samples, download chapters, and find quick answers when you need the most accurate, current information. Try it for free at *http://safari.oreilly.com*.

Acknowledgments

Thanks to Paul Allen (the Younger), whose blog inspired me to see the importance of the Facebook Platform. Thanks to Allan Young and Phil Burns for inspiring me to quit my day job and truly get out on my own. Big thanks to Joseph Scott, who somehow had enough faith in me to introduce me to O'Reilly. Thanks to Elizabeth, Thomas, Joseph, and Jesse III for dealing without a daddy for a short time while I wrote this book. Most of all, I'd like to thank Rebecca, who endured childbirth the day before this was sent off for review, lots of late nights, and dealing with four kids so I could finish writing.

CHAPTER 1
"Hello Friends"

The "Hello World" for Social Development

I generally cringe when I see "Hello World" examples in modern books on software development. It's been used so often that it almost doesn't teach anything anymore. However, because the social Web brings a new layer to web development, I'd like to show you a new layer to the "Hello World" example. A social application is all about interaction—it's about establishing a conversation with your friends.

When writing social applications, you have to consider the fact that, in a way, you're having a conversation with the people you are writing software for. Not only must your application talk to your users, but it must also allow them to talk to you and to each other. Simply taking an existing website and putting it on a social site such as Facebook will not bring you millions of users in weeks or months like the apps described in this chapter. Your Facebook application must give users the ability to share their actions with friends, broadcast to the world, find people with similar interests, and most of all, identify themselves in ways they never could before on traditional websites. Instead of asking yourself, "How will my users utilize my application?," you should now ask yourself, "How will my users' friends utilize my application?"

The following list shows some examples of several applications on Facebook, all with 100,000 daily active users or more at the time of this writing. Examine them and see if you can figure out why they have become as popular as they are. Then, apply those features to your own Facebook application design:

iLike
(http://www.facebook.com/apps/application.php?id=2413267546&b)
: I can't tell you the number of clients who come to me asking for an application "just like iLike." iLike has all the elements of a good Facebook app, allowing you to track the songs you're listening to and share them

with your friends on Facebook. This is the ultimate example of an external website that successfully integrated into Facebook.

Scrabulous (http://www.facebook.com/apps/application.php?id=3052170175&b)
: The ultimate social game on Facebook! This app allows you to challenge your Facebook friends to Scrabble™, track your progress, and share your progress with others. This is something you could invite your grandma to play.

Likeness (http://www.facebook.com/apps/application.php?id=2405948328&b)
: Find out what celebrity, singer, or artist you are like, and then share it with your friends.

Honesty Box (http://apps.facebook.com/apps/application.php?id=2552096927&b)
: This app provides an anonymous way for your friends to say things about you without you knowing who said them.

Circle of Friends (http://apps.facebook.com/apps/application.php?id=2270425051&b)
: Find new friends with similar likes and interests, and share things with them.

As you can see from these examples, simplicity is key when integrating social elements into your application. We are going to start simple, too: we'll create a simple application using just FBML that says "hello" to you and allows you to invite your friends to use it. The application we create here can be found at *http://apps.facebook.com/fbmlessentials*. All examples throughout this book will be added as components of this Facebook application so that you can see the results of what we are developing.

Step 1: Set Up a Facebook Developer Account

The first step in creating a Facebook app is to register a developer account. Of course, you can develop applications using your normal Facebook account, but then you risk potentially exposing your app to competitors and others while it's still under development. It is generally better practice to always develop and test your app in an account designated as a developer on Facebook. To set up a developer account, do the following:

1. Log out of your normal Facebook account.
2. On the Facebook home page, click the "Sign Up" button:

Sign Up

3. Fill in the form with any information you want. This could be completely fake, as it will be only your developer account, not your main account.
4. Submit the form, and wait for a confirmation email. In the email, click on the link. You're now logged into your new account!
5. Now that you're logged in, copy this URL into your browser's URL bar: *http://www.facebook.com/developers/become_test_account.php*
6. On the next screen, click on the "Make [*your developer username*] a Test Account" button:

Become a Platform Application Test Account

You are logged in as Jesse Stay.

Test accounts should not be used to interact with normal Facebook users. If you do so, your account may be disabled.

Make Jesse Stay a Test Account

7. That will take you to a final confirmation page. Congratulations, you now have a developer account! Remember the email address you used for this account, as you'll need it to log in every time you want to test your app.

Don't follow these steps using your real account or you will lose very important functionality!

Step 2: Add the Developer App

1. This step is simple. To add the developer app, in your developer account click on "Developers."
2. On the subsequent page, click on "Get Started" in pink.
3. Click on the "Add Facebook Developer Application" button:

   Add Facebook Developer Application

   Or you can just copy this link and skip the process above: *http://www.facebook.com/developers*
4. Leave everything checked, and click "Add Developer."
5. You now have the developer app installed and can begin creating applications on Facebook. You'll notice a new "Developer" link on the left now.

Step 3: Set Up the App

1. Click on the "Developer" link on the left in your developer account.
2. That should take you to the Developer page. Click on "Set Up New Application."
3. You now have the opportunity to enter an application name. We'll call this app "FBML Essentials". Click on the checkbox:

   Application Name (Limit: 50 characters) FBML Essentials

   ☑ Check here to indicate that you have read and agree to the terms of the Facebook Platform.

4. Click on "Optional Fields," and more form fields should become available to you. Here are the optional fields and what they will do:

   Developer Contact Email
   : This is the email address Facebook will use if it ever needs to contact you about your application. For this example app, we will enter *admin@fbmlessentials.staynalive.com*.

   User Support Email
   : On your app's Help page, users can send support requests. Requests from that page will be sent to the address you set here. We'll enter *support@fbmlessentials.staynalive.com* for this app.

   Callback URL
   : The callback URL is the anchor for your entire application. All Facebook requests get forwarded to this URL behind the scenes. For the purposes of this app, we'll use *http://fbmlessentials.staynalive.com*. You will want to enter the URL of your own website, one that you control. It is important to add a trailing slash to this URL because all requests to *http://apps.facebook.com/fbmlessentials* (see the "Canvas Page URL" field, next) get translated to this URL behind the scenes, and adding a slash ensures that the URL *http://apps.facebook.com/fbmlessentials/foo.php* does not end up becoming something like *http://fbmlessentials.staynalive.comfoo.php*.

   Canvas Page URL
   : There is one box here that follows *apps.facebook.com*. The text you enter in this box must be unique and unused by other Facebook app developers. For the purposes of this app, we'll enter "fbmlessentials" in the box, which means that the canvas page URL will be *http://apps.facebook.com/fbmlessentials*. (You'll want to choose your own when working on your own app, of course.) If the address is available, it will say "available" next to the box.

Use FBML (or Use iframe)
: This goes back to the "unofficial" developer guidelines we discussed earlier in the Preface. Rarely do you want to make your entire application an iframe. Although that gives you more flexibility for highly intensive JavaScript or Flash applications, it keeps you from valuable uses of FBML. I suggest you select "Use FBML" and use the `<fb:iframe/>` tag (described in Chapter 3) to insert rich JavaScript applications into your Facebook app. For the purposes of this app, we'll select "Use FBML."

Application Type
: This can be "Website" or "Desktop." "Desktop" enables the application for use outside of a web environment. For the purposes of this app, however, we're going to select "Website."

Mobile Integration
: Check this option if you need your app to use mobile features on Facebook. This enables SMS and mobile browser viewing. For now, leave this unchecked.

IP Addresses of Servers Making Requests
: This is a comma-separated list of IP addresses of your servers that might be communicating with Facebook. This is a great security feature, but for this app, we'll leave this blank.

Can Your Application be added on Facebook?
: Sometimes you may not need the user to add your application to Facebook in order to use it. If this is the case, you can choose "No" here. For this app, choose "Yes," and a new set of installation options will become available to you. (See step 5 for more details.)

TOS URL
: This is an optional URL that, if entered, forces the user to click a link to accept a Terms of Service (TOS) agreement if they want to install the app. We'll leave this blank for now.

Developers
: You must add other developers as friends in your account before you can add them here. Once they are your friends, you can select any of them to be allowed to work on and install your application while it is under development.

5. If you selected "Yes" to the "Can Your Application be added on Facebook?" option in the previous step, a new section called "Installation Options" will appear. Here are your choices (all are optional) and what they mean:

Who can add your application to their Facebook account?
: You have the option to choose between "Users," "All Pages," "Some Pages," and "No Pages." Checking "Users" enables any user to add the app to their profile. Selecting "All Pages" enables any user to add the app to any page on Facebook. Selecting "Some Pages" allows you to specify a certain type of Facebook page that your app can be added to. For the purposes of this app, we'll check "Users" and leave "No Pages" selected. The result is that this app can be added only to user profiles.

Post-Add URL
: This is the URL to which your application gets redirected after a user adds the app. This can be a great place to encourage a user to sign up or add friends. For this app, we'll enter *http://apps.facebook.com/fbmlessentials/invite.php* in this field.

Application Description
: When a user adds your application, this text appears on the page asking the user to add the application. For this app, we'll just enter "FBML Essentials Demo Application."

Post-Remove URL
: A non-*Facebook.com* URL, this is a place to redirect the user after the user removes your app, which will notify your application that it has been removed. This can be a great way to disable a user's account in your database for tracking purposes. We'll leave this blank for this app.

Default FBML
: Unless an API method is called through server-side code, this is the default text that appears on a user's profile under the application's profile box. It can contain most FBML tags in addition to text. Here is where our first "Hello World" example comes into play. Enter the following in this box:

```
Hello <fb:name uid="loggedinuser" useyou="false" />
```

What just happened? You'll see this later, but after the application has been added, "Hello [*user's name*]" will appear in the application's profile box in your user profile. `<fb:name/>` is an FBML tag that calls the name of the Facebook ID specified by `uid`. For this example, we enter `loggedinuser` as the `uid`. This means that the name of the person visiting your profile will be rendered by the tag. `useyou="false"` means that if you're visiting your own profile, it doesn't say "Hello you," but rather, "Hello [*your name*]".

Default Action FBML[*]
: This optional field should be a link that appears under the profile picture of the user who installed the app. This must be an absolute URL. For the purposes of this app, enter:

```
<fb:profile-action url='http://apps.facebook.com/fbmlessentials/
    invite.php'> Invite <fb:name uid="profileowner"
    useyou="false" /> to use FBML Essentials!
</fb:profile-action>
```

You'll see how this looks on a user's profile later in this chapter.

What just happened? `<fb:profile-action/>` sets a link under a user's profile image. In fact, it will also place a link on all of the user's friends' profile pages (visible only when the person who has installed your app views those profiles).

Default Profile Box Column
: You have two options here: "Wide" or "Narrow." For the small amount of text we're displaying, we'll select "Narrow" for this app.

Developer Mode
: When you are developing an app that you don't want others to install or see until you are finished, select this option. If you'd like, you can add other developers who can test the app. Just don't forget to uncheck this box when you go live! For this example app, it's your choice whether to select this option.

6. Along with "Installation Options," a section called "Integration Points" appears (these are also optional):

[*] Note that this will probably be deprecated when the new Facebook design is launched.

Side Nav URL
: If you want a link to appear on the lefthand side of the page when you are logged into your Facebook account, you will need to enter an *apps.facebook.com* URL in this box. For this application, we will enter *http://apps.facebook.com/fbmlessentials*.

Privacy URL
: This can be any URL. In FBML, you can specify the insertion of a privacy link. The contents of this field will be the location to which the privacy link takes the user. For this app, we'll leave it blank.

Help URL
: This can be any URL. In FBML, you can specify the insertion of a help link (similar to the privacy URL). The contents of this field will be the location to which the help link takes the user. For this app, we'll leave it blank.

Private Installation
: When developing a Facebook application, there may be times when you don't want others to know you are working on it. Check this box to prevent information about the app from appearing in your friends' News and Mini-Feeds. For this app, this box is optional.

Attachments – Attachment Action
: This action can be text or FBML. It appears when a user wants to add an attachment to a Wall post or message. We'll leave this blank for this app.

Attachments – Callback URL
: A non-*apps.facebook.com* URL that loads the content to be attached to a Wall post or message. We'll leave this blank for this app.

Hit "Submit," and you've created your first application! Let's add it and see what it looks like. On the resulting page after you hit "Submit," find your application and click "View About Page." Now, click "Add Application." On the following page, leave everything checked and click the button to add the app.

The app will send you to the *invite.php* page we saw earlier (in the Default Action FBML option). You will get a message similar to this:

Errors while loading page from application

Received HTTP error code 404 while loading
http://fbmlessentials.staynalive.com/invite.php?auth_token=

This is because we haven't set anything for *invite.php* yet. We'll create that shortly. Now, click on your "Profile" link in the upper-left corner. Under your profile image, you'll see an image similar to this:

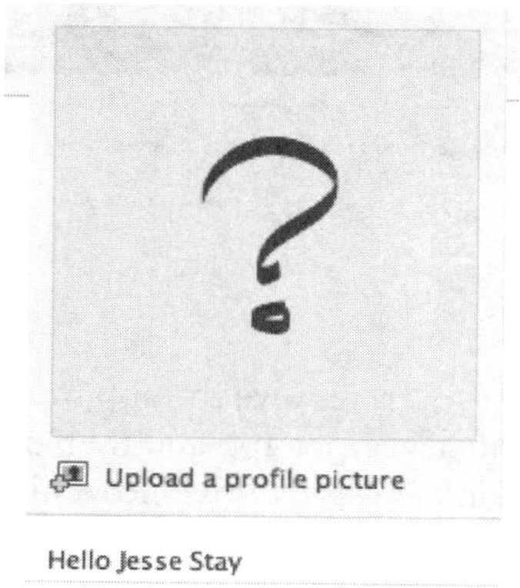

And further down on the page, you'll see a box similar to this:

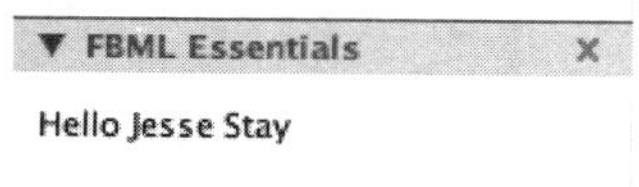

Now, create an *index.html* or *index.php* file in the home directory where your callback URL is. Place the following in that file:

```
Hello <fb:name uid="loggedinuser" useyou="false" />
```

Next, open the file you specified earlier in the Post-Add URL option (we used *invite.php*), and add the following text (substituting your own information where necessary, including replacing *.php* with *.html* if you used *index.html*):

```
<fb:request-form action="index.php" method="POST" invite="true"
     type="FBML Essentials" content="Hello Friend. <fb:req-choice
     url='http://apps.facebook.com/fbmlessentials' label='Go there!'/>">
        <fb:multi-friend-selector showborder="false" actiontext="Invite
            your friends to use FBML Essentials.">
</fb:request-form>
```

Click on the link to your new Facebook app in the left sidebar of your Facebook account (or just click on the "Hello [*your name*]" link under your profile image!). You'll now get a page like this:

facebook
Profile edit
Friends
Networks
Inbox
home
Hello Jesse Stay
Search
Applications
edit
Photos
Page built by FBML Essentials
Advertisers
Businesses
Developers

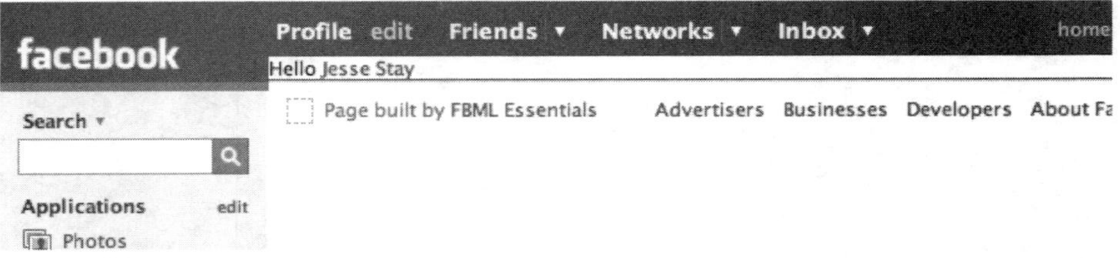

If you click on the "FBML Essentials" link in the footer, remove the app from your profile, and then re-add it (by clicking on the developer app and then on your new app), and you'll see the invite page again. This time it will look like this:

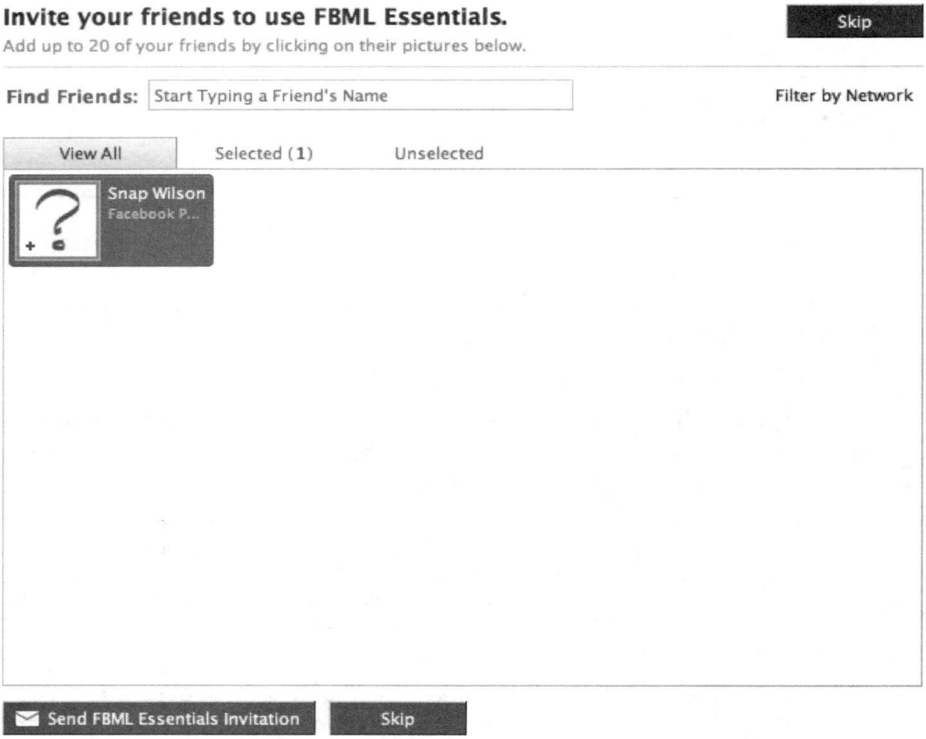

Invite your friends to use FBML Essentials.
Add up to 20 of your friends by clicking on their pictures below.
Skip
Find Friends:
Start Typing a Friend's Name
Filter by Network
View All
Selected (1)
Unselected
Snap Wilson
Facebook P...
Send FBML Essentials Invitation
Skip

Now, if you have added any friends, select them here and choose "Send [*your app name*] Invitation." You'll be prompted to verify the invitation. Hit "Send," and an invitation will be sent to the users you just selected, asking them to add the app to their profiles. Congratulations—you have just written your first app, all in FBML. Hello friends!

What just happened? The text or FBML you enter in your *index.html* or *index.php* gets loaded with the callback URL you entered previously in the application setup screen. In *invite.php*, we used the `<fb:request-form/>` and `<fb:multi-friend-selector/>` tags to create an automatically generated invite form for your users to invite their friends. With these tags, Facebook does all the work for you in making your app viral! Because we added *invite.php* to the Post-Add URL field in the setup, the application will always be directed there after the user adds the app. This can be a great way to encourage your users to add your app to Facebook.

In the next chapter, I will go over a few design considerations you need to remember when planning out your FBML-based Facebook application. We'll cover some architecture options you'll need to incorporate into your design, as well as basic HTML design in an FBML environment.

CHAPTER 2

HTML Design in a Facebook Environment

HTML on an FBML-parsed page renders in just the same way that the FBML renders. On the whole, most HTML tags in the Facebook environment will render the same as normal HTML. However, for the developer's benefit, as well as for the security and protection of your app, and to integrate better with the Facebook environment, Facebook parses a few tags differently than your normal HTML. This chapter covers a few things to be aware of when designing your Facebook application in FBML.

Forms in FBML

Forms in FBML are almost the same as forms in HTML, but when rendered by Facebook, they produce a few more hidden input fields. The following section covers the specs for the form tag.

The <form/> tag

The form tag renders a form in HTML, adding five additional hidden input fields—the `fb_sig_profile`, `fb_sig_user`, `fb_sig_session_key`, `fb_sig_time`, and `fb_sig` parameters—that give more information about the user submitting the form to the processing script. The `fb_sig` parameter is essentially just a hash (see *http://en.wikipedia.org/wiki/Hash_algorithm*) of all the other `fb_sig_` values preceding it.

It is important to note that the `fb_sig_user` and `fb_sig_session_key` parameters are added only if the user using your app has successfully authenticated and logged into Facebook.

FBML-Specific Attributes

```
requirelogin=[true|false] default: true
```

If `true`, the user will be prompted to log in (if they have not already done so), and then they will be asked if they want to submit data to your app. The login redirects the user to the posted form, with the `fb_sig_user` and `fb_sig_session` values attached to that form.

The following optional attributes can be applied to any form element within the form:

`clicktoenable=[`*`element id`*`]`
: When added to any element within a form, this enables the element specified by ***`element id`*** when the current element is clicked. Multiple element IDs can be submitted if they are separated by commas.

`clicktodisable=[`*`element id`*`]`
: When added to any element within a form, this disables the element specified by ***`element id`*** when the current element is clicked. Multiple element IDs can be submitted if they are separated by commas.

`clickthrough=[true|false] default: false`
: When added to any element within a form in which Dynamic FBML (such as the previous attributes, or Mock AJAX or Visibility attributes) is being used, and if it is set to `true`, this attribute allows the original form element functionality to occur. One example use is for checkboxes. When `clicktoenable`, `clicktodisable`, or any of the Visibility attributes are used on a checkbox element, by default the checkbox will not get checked. Setting `clickthrough=true` fixes this issue.

Example FBML

The following example demonstrates the form tag, where `clicktodisable` and `clickthrough` are used together (refer to *http://wiki.developers.facebook.com/index.php/DynamicFBML/Forms*):

```
<form>
  <input type="text" id="firstname" name="firstname" />
  <input id="sendbutton" type="submit" value="Submit"
     clicktodisable="firstname" clicktohide="sendbutton"
     clickthrough="true" />
</form>
```

Rendered HTML for Single Instance of Tag

The following is the rendered HTML for the example just shown (refer to *http://wiki.developers.facebook.com/index.php/UsageNotes/Forms*):

```
<form>
  <input type="hidden" name="fb_sig_profile" value="1160"/>
  <input type="hidden" name="fb_sig_user" value="1160"/>
  <input type="hidden" name="fb_sig_session_key"
      value="b12d7f73fc47536b32e89e-1160"/>
  <input type="hidden" name="fb_sig_time" value="1176705186"/>
  <input type="hidden" name="fb_sig"
      value="773af1263c2b7bade7958e6b58d3152f"/>
  ...
</form>
```

Additional information

- Any `<input/>` element added by the user cannot have a name that starts with `fb`. Names that start with `fb` are reserved by Facebook.
- If you are uploading a file through a form, the form must not be posted to an *apps.facebook.com* domain. Instead, your form should be submitted to your own servers' domain, and your servers should redirect the user back to the *apps.facebook.com* domain after saving the file.
- See the section on Mock AJAX in Chapter 3 to learn how you can dynamically load submitted form results into an additional `<div/>` tag on the page using AJAX.
- Any form element that is disabled does not get submitted to the form.
- When used together, the `clickthrough` and `clicktodisable` tags don't allow a form to submit in Apple's Safari 3 browser. This bug has been submitted to Safari.

Images in FBML

All images in FBML get cached by Facebook's servers. Facebook makes a request to your application, and as your application serves up `<img/>` tags, Facebook parses those images, ensures that they aren't too big and that they meet various requirements, and then stores a copy of each image on the Facebook servers. From that point on, the cached version of your image on Facebook's servers gets rendered by your browser, which saves your own servers from unneeded bandwidth costs.

Your images must be smaller than 50 MB, cannot be animated, and cannot be served as a script (a common method to track a cookie or even serve malicious code). This ensures quality among applications and keeps Facebook users feeling safe and secure when using your app. Images must be given as an absolute link to the callback URL that you specified in your application installation settings (described in Chapter 1).

If the cache of your image does not work for some reason, Facebook renders a blank image in your application. If you need to refresh your image from the Facebook cache, it is recommended you get your hands dirty with some actual Facebook API code. Look up the `facebook.fbml.refreshImgSrc()` API tag on the Facebook Developer Wiki for more information about how to do this (see *http://developers.facebook.com/documentation.php?v=1.0&method=fbml.refreshImgSrc*).

Facebook also recommends that application developers do not append cache breaking strings (random strings to break the image cache) to the end of their URLs. This ensures that if your image ever actually does change, there is only one version of your image on Facebook's servers to update. It will also keep the load off your servers.

CSS and DOM in FBML

CSS in FBML can be tricky if you don't recognize the quirks associated with it. FBML supports `<link/>` tags for importing external files into your rendered HTML, as well as `style` attributes and `<style/>` tags for rendering the CSS inline. One must recognize, however, that Facebook reads these external files and parses them into its own formats.

Facebook treats `<link/>` tags very similarly to `<img/>` references in that, on first load of the file, it stores a cached copy of the file on the Facebook servers. The difference is that once the file is cached, that file never gets deleted. Therefore, it might be wise to append a `?version=2.0` or similar parameter if you want to indicate the file was changed. URLs in a `<link/>` href attribute must be absolute, just like `<img/>` tags, and must link to the callback URL specified in the application's installation settings.

Here's an example `<link/>` tag in FBML (referring back to our "Hello World" application in Chapter 1):

```
<link rel="stylesheet" type="text/css" href="http://fbmlessentials.
    staynalive.com/facebook.css?version=1.0" />
```

CSS within your FBML, whether it's within `<style/>` tags or documents linked from `<link/>` tags, must adhere to certain guidelines. Facebook, when reading `id` attributes in the DOM from your HTML, rewrites those IDs with the string `app`, appended by the ID of your application, followed by an underscore, and then the original ID you specified. The following HTML that you send to Facebook through your app:

```
<div id="foo">bar</div>
```

gets rendered by Facebook as:

```
<div id="app0123456789_foo">bar</div>
```

Therefore, in your CSS, all rules for IDs (those prefixed by #) must have the app0123456789_ prefixed to the ID. Which means:

```
#foo { ... }
```

should be:

```
#app0123456789_foo { ... }
```

in your CSS <style/> element or file. Take some time to practice these examples. Improper CSS and prefixing with application IDs in the wrong places have been the cause of some of the largest headaches I've had when using FBML.

As a reference, see Table 2-1 for a list of the default CSS styles for each of the major HTML elements in Facebook. Every time you insert one of these HTML elements, the associated CSS gets assigned to that HTML element. This is important to remember as you are trying to assign your own CSS to these elements.

Table 2-1. Default CSS properties for elements on a Facebook canvas page

HTML element	CSS properties
<body/>, <p/>	font-family: lucida grande, tahoma, verdana, arial, sans-serif; font-size: 11px
<h1/>	color: #333; font-size: 14px
<h2/>, <h3/>	color: #333; font-size: 13px
<h4/>, <h5/>	color: #333; font-size: 11px
<a/>	color: #3B5998; text-decoration: none
a:hover	text-decoration: underline
<img/>	border: 0px none
<select/>	border: 1px solid #BDC7D8
<input/>	border-color: #ADADAD; border-style: solid; border-width: 1px

JavaScript in FBML

Facebook provides an FBML-specific version of JavaScript parsing called FBJS (Facebook JavaScript). This helps protect and not confuse the external scripts Facebook uses on the rest of its site. (We'll cover FBJS in much more detail in Chapter 4.) Facebook wants to maintain security on profile pages so that users don't get inundated with music, videos, and pop ups right when they visit a profile page.

Similar to `<link/>` tags in CSS, you can load external JavaScript files through `<script/>` tags that get cached in exactly the same way as `<link/>` tags. For example, to load external JavaScript, you would load a `<script/>` tag such as the following:

```
<script src="http://fbmlessentials.staynalive.com/facebook.js?version=
    1.0"></script>
```

Calls to the `<script/>` tag are limited to canvas pages only. Profile boxes can use FBJS, but they must be called with inline JavaScript rather than by an external JavaScript file.

Here are some rules regarding FBJS:

- Methods are prepended with `app`, followed by the application ID of your app and an underscore. Be sure when referencing the method later to reference the parsed method name instead of your original method name. Global functions provided by Facebook are not rewritten in this manner.
- Only the `onclick` attribute is supported in FBML/HTML elements for your app. To access other events for your FBML/HTML, you must set up an event listener.
- Profile FBJS only activates after a user performs some sort of click action in the application's profile box. This prevents music, pop ups, and other things happening without the user's permission when visiting another user's profile page.

Other Things to Consider

Thus far, we've covered most of the basic HTML techniques you need to consider when writing your Facebook application. In the following sections, we'll cover a few more miscellaneous techniques and caveats that you will want to know as you are developing your app.

User IDs and FBML

User IDs supplied to FBML are 64-bit integers created by Facebook to identify each user. You might notice when you visit your Facebook profile that the URL is structured like this: *http://www.facebook.com/profile.php?id=683545112*.

The number after the *id=* is your Facebook ID. When planning your app, you may want to store this ID in a database for later reference. In MySQL, I use the `BIGINT(20)` data type to do this. You will want to find the equivalent for your database environment.

In addition to the ID, whenever there is a `uid` attribute in FBML, you can use the following identifiers in place of the actual ID of the user:

`loggedinuser`
: Returns the Facebook ID of the user who is visiting the profile or canvas page on which your app is installed.

`profileowner`
: Returns the Facebook ID of the user who has actually installed your app (the profile owner), not the visiting user.

Public Canvas Pages and SEO

By default, your application's canvas page is publicly searchable by search engines and viewable by those not logged into Facebook. This makes it very important to ensure that your application's canvas pages are tuned for Search Engine Optimization (SEO), so that others can use your app outside Facebook or are at least encouraged to log in and use your application.

All FBML is built to work on canvas pages even when the user is not logged in. To force a user to be logged in before using your app, use the `<fb:is-logged-out/>` tag, described in the next section.

The <fb:is-logged-out/> tag

This tag enables only certain content to be viewable if the user is logged out. If the user is logged in, the content between the `<fb:else/>` tags is rendered. Note that `<fb:is-logged-out/>` has no FBML-specific attributes.

Example FBML

The following example demonstrates the `<fb:is-logged-out/>` tag:

```
<fb:is-logged-out>
  Any FBML can go here for the user only when the user is not logged in.
  <fb:else>
    When the user is logged in, any FBML can be used here.
  </fb:else>
</fb:is-logged-out>
```

Rendered HTML for Single Instance of Tag

If the user is not logged in to Facebook, the text "Any FBML can go here for the user only when the user is not logged in" will appear. If the user is logged in to Facebook, the text "When the user is logged in, any FBML can be used here" will appear.

Additional information

Both inside and outside the `<fb:is-logged-out/>` tag, the tags in the following table are rendered differently, depending on whether the user is logged in or not.

Tag	Logged-in behavior	Logged-out behavior
`<fb:if/>`	Content within `<fb:if/>` block is rendered.	Content within `<fb:else/>` block is rendered.
`<fb:name/>`	Renders the full name of the user (by default).	Renders only the user's first name, regardless of attributes passed to the tag.
`<fb:profile-pic/>`	Renders the user's profile picture.	Renders the user's profile picture only if the user's preferences state to do so for logged-out users. Otherwise, a question mark is displayed to non-logged-in users.

Hosting

"Where is the best place to host?" is one of the biggest questions I hear from my clients who want to build Facebook applications for their businesses. With a traditional web application, traffic buildup is gradual because you are dealing with a new audience in a nonviral channel for building hype for your website. On Facebook, however, the situation is different. With a good idea and the right viral elements in place, some applications have gone from zero page views to hundreds of millions in a matter of days. Without the proper infrastructure in place to handle this kind of traffic, your app could go down within minutes and your maximum potential for spreading the application could go out the door.

There are two hosting services at the time of this writing that I suggest you look into. I won't go into detail, but these services provide a means of quick scaling as traffic to your application increases. The first—and my preference—is Amazon EC2 (Elastic Compute Cloud) combined with S3 (Simple Storage Service) for backups. EC2 gives you a very fast way to programmatically scale your app as needed, while requiring you to pay only for the bandwidth and servers you need. The second service is Joyent. Joyent provides speedy scaling to new servers as needed, and it provides a direct line to Facebook so that your applications will have the fastest connection possible to Facebook's servers. Beyond those two suggestions, of course, you can always find a good hosting center if you know what you're doing and negotiate your prices as you need to scale. Just be prepared to have some servers of your own ready as a backup!

Once you have selected your service, what's the best way to set up your servers to prepare for an influx of traffic such as I mentioned? That would take an entire book to detail, but my best suggestion is to keep your data as persistent as possible, so that if you need to fire up another instance of your server, it can automatically know where to retrieve the data. I strongly recommend hiring a good system administrator if this is not something you think you can handle, and at least have him on hand to prepare for the event of heavy traffic.

The Facebook Platform Architecture

When you visit any application on Facebook, it looks just as though it were being hosted right on the Facebook servers. In reality, Facebook is simply a proxy, reading the browser requests, passing them onto your servers, reading your servers' responses, and then parsing that information back to the user in HTML format (see Figure 2-1).

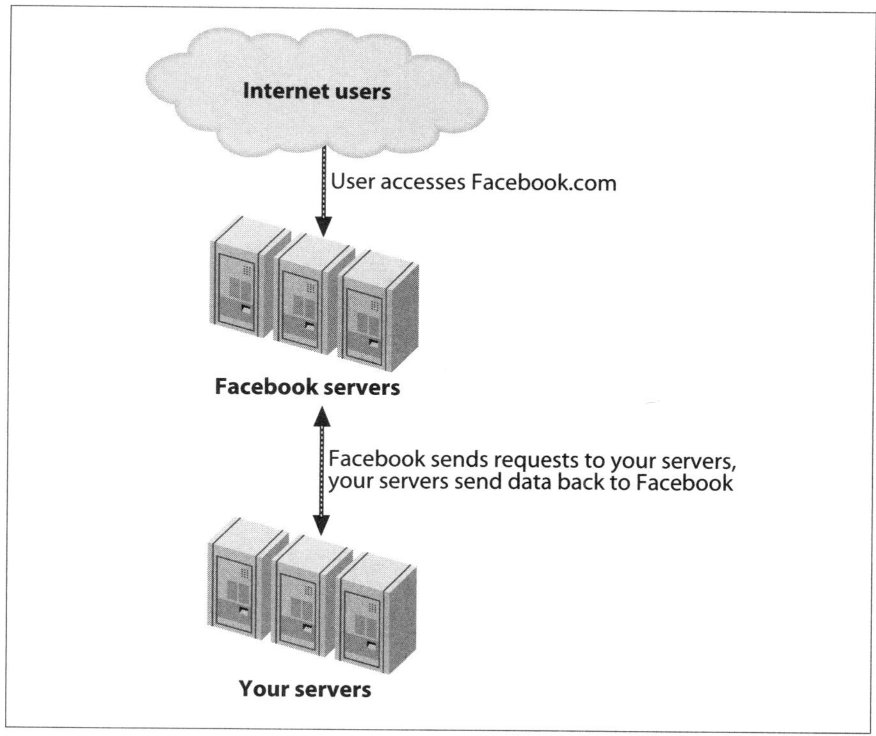

Figure 2-1. When you access a Facebook app, you are actually talking to Facebook's servers, which in turn communicate back to your servers

The one exception to this process is when data is rendered within an iframe. iframes on Facebook are not parsed by Facebook, so they allow you to do almost anything you want without worrying whether Facebook is able to parse the data you are providing. iframes have their limitations, however, because FBML is not possible in an iframe! I'll explain more of those limitations in the `<fb:iframe/>` section in Chapter 3.

Chapter 3 is intended to be a reference to FBML. In it, I will include examples of the code you'll be writing and show you what these examples render. I hope you'll be able to refer back frequently to the next chapter as you continue your development on Facebook.

CHAPTER 3
FBML Reference

Throughout this chapter, I'll cover the details of FBML, every single tag available at the time of this writing, and how each tag works. Please refer back to this chapter often as you write your FBML.

Let's start by showing how you can test these tags in your own browser without the need of a web server.

Facebook FBML Test Console

The Facebook FBML Test Console is an invaluable tool for any Facebook developer to test his FBML tags before putting them into production. Because Facebook has no true sandbox environment, every change to your application that you publish is available for any of your users to see (unless you have two versions of the same application, which is what a lot of developers end up doing). To help you avoid making errors in the Facebook Platform before your code goes live, Facebook has provided a test console for your FBML so that you can see what your code will look like when it gets rendered by Facebook.

To use this console, simply go to the Facebook developers website at *http://developers.facebook.com* and click on "Tools" in the top navigation. You'll see a series of test consoles you can play with. These include a console for the API, another for previewing the feeds you create, and—the one we're concerned with here—the FBML Test Console. Click on the "FBML Test Console" tab, and now you can test to your heart's content! If you want to skip these steps, this link will take you straight there: *http://developers.facebook.com/tools.php?fbml*.

The FBML Test Console enables you to specify any profile ID, any application API key, and any set of HTML, FBJS, and/or FBML code so that you can see how Facebook will render it. When you enter a bit of FBML code and click "Preview," you will be shown the browser output, along with the rendered HTML and any errors for that output. See Figure 3-1.

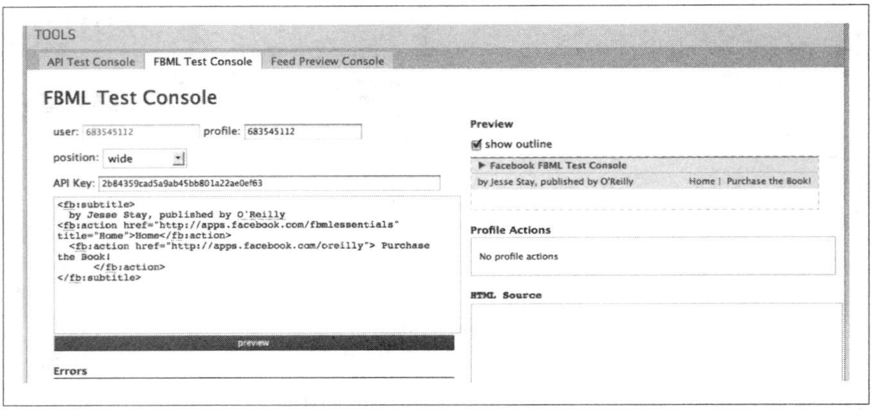

Figure 3-1. The FBML Test Console

The rest of this chapter will serve as a reference for you as you write your FBML. I suggest reading through the chapter and trying out each of the tags in the FBML Test Console to see what they produce. There may be times when you don't want to use FBML but instead want to reproduce what the FBML would do as HTML. The Test Console is ideal for that. Practice using the tags described in this chapter with the FBML Test Console, and soon you'll be a pro!

Authorization Tags

Each of the following tags verify in some way the permissions for a user's role on Facebook. These tags can be quite useful for virally promoting your app. For instance, if you want to encourage non-app users to install your app, use the `<fb:visible-to-added-app-users/>` tag in your application's profile box to provide a message that encourages non-app users to add your application. Or, if you want to provide an admin interface that allows the owner of an app or the admin of a page to administer settings within your app, use the `<fb:if-is-user/>` tag with a `uid` of `profileowner`, and only the user who added your app will have access to those settings.

In this section, we will define the specifications of each authorization-related FBML tag on Facebook. The first half of the tags render only on a user's canvas page or on a canvas page for a Facebook Page. The second half of the tags render only on a user's profile or on a Facebook Page; they will not render on a canvas page. Each section in this chapter includes a brief description of the tag, followed by required and optional attributes that can be passed to the tags, as well as examples of how those tags can be used.

The "User" Authorization Tag

<fb:user/>

```
<fb:user uid="...">...</fb:user>
```

Depending on the user's privacy settings, the content rendered within this tag displays only to users who actually have permission to see that user's profile.

FBML-Specific Attributes

Required

`uid=[`*`string`*`]`
: The ID of the user to protect content for.

Optional

None.

Example FBML

Here is example FBML code for a user whose information you would like to protect:

```
<fb:user id="4">
The content rendered here will only display if you have permission to
    view Mark Zuckerberg's Profile.
</fb:user>
```

Rendered HTML for Single Instance of Tag

If you have permission to see Mark Zuckerberg's profile, the following will appear where you place the FBML example just shown:

```
The content rendered here will only display if you have permission to
view Mark Zuckerberg's Profile.
```

Of course, if you don't have permission to see Mark Zuckerberg's profile, nothing will appear where the `<fb:user/>` tag is placed.

Authorizing by User Agent

<fb:user-agent/>

`<fb:user-agent [includes="..."|excludes="..."]>...</fb:user-agent>`

Renders the content within the tags only if it is viewed with the specified browser or browsers. You can also use this tag so that content renders only if it is viewed in all browsers except a specified browser or browsers.

FBML-Specific Attributes

Required

This tag must contain at least one or both of the following attributes:

`includes=[`*`comma-separated list of one or more user agents`*`] default: none`
: Specified group of browsers to display content for. Accepts either one value or a comma-separated list of values. See *http://www.user-agents.org/index.shtml* for a list of user-agent strings that can be used here.

`excludes=[`*`comma-separated list of one or more user agents`*`] default: none`
: The network ID (`nid`) to test against. If the user is not in this network, either the content within the `<fb:else/>` tags is rendered or no content is rendered at all.

Optional

None.

Example FBML

Let's say you want to render a message only to users of Mozilla Firefox. You would write your FBML code like this:

```
<fb:user-agent includes="firefox">
    We love Firefox users!
</fb:user-agent>
```

If you want to render a message to everyone except Internet Explorer (IE) users, you would write this:

```
<fb:user-agent excludes="ie">
    You picked a great browser that works well with our app!
</fb:user-agent>
```

To get really tricky, let's display a message to all IE users except those who use IE 5.0:

```
<fb:user-agent includes="ie" excludes="ie 5">
    We like all versions of IE, except version 5.
</fb:user-agent>
```

Rendered HTML for Single Instance of Tag

So, for the first example just shown, let's say you're a Firefox user and you visit the app. The following message would be displayed:

```
We love Firefox users!
```

All other browsers would display nothing. For the second example, if you were using an Internet Explorer-based browser, the app would show nothing. However, all other browsers would show this:

```
You picked a great browser that works well with our app!
```

The third example would not display anything unless you were using a version of Internet Explorer other than version 5.0. All other versions of Internet Explorer would display this:

```
We like all versions of IE, except version 5.
```

Additional Information

- When both includes and excludes are used together, the order of priority is includes first, then excludes.
- You can use shortcuts for the most common user-agent strings, but Facebook's documentation leaves it unclear what these shortcuts are other than "ie," "firefox," and "mozilla." You seem to be able to treat the names broadly—as long as the user-agent name contains the shortcut that you enter, it is considered a match and should work. As more information about this tag comes to light, I will update this book's Facebook Page (*http://page.fbmlessentials.com*).

Canvas Page Authorization Tags

It's important to note that most of the canvas page authorization tags listed in this section are compatible with the `<fb:else/>` tag.

<fb:is-in-network/>

```
<fb:is-in-network>...<fb:else>...</fb:else></fb:is-in-network>
```

Content within the tags is rendered only if the user is in the specified network. Use the `<fb:else/>` logic tag (described later in this chapter) to render content if a user is not in the specified network.

FBML-Specific Attributes

Required

`network=[int] default: none`
: The network ID (`nid`) to test against. If the user is not in this network, either the content within the `<fb:else/>` tags is rendered or no content is rendered at all.

Optional

`uid=[int] default: loggedinuser`
: The user ID to test the network against.

Example FBML

Here is example FBML code for `<fb:is-in-network/>`:

```
<fb:is-in-network network="1234567890" uid="0987654321">

    This text shows up if user with id 0987654321 is in
    the network with id 1234567890.

  <fb:else>

    If user with id 0987654321 is not in network with id
    1234567890 this text will show up.

  </fb:else>

</fb:is-in-network>
```

Additional Information

- This tag supports `<fb:else/>` even though it does not start with `<fb:if*/>`.
- This tag works only on canvas pages and feed stories. It will not work on profiles, notifications, or News Feeds.

<fb:if-can-see/>

`<fb:if-can-see>...<fb:else>...</fb:else></fb:if-can-see>`

Looks at a given user's privacy settings and verifies, based on data provided to the `what` attribute, whether a user has permission to see the enclosed content. Use the `<fb:else/>` tag (described later in this chapter) to display content if a user does not have permission to display the enclosed content. `<fb:if-can-see/>` can be an excellent way to provide your own privacy controls on your application.

FBML-Specific Attributes

Required

`uid=[int] default: none`

The user ID to test privacy settings against.

Optional

`what=[profile|friends|not_limited|online|statusupdates|wall|groups|courses|photosofme|notes|feed|contact|email|aim|cell|phone|mailbox|address|basic|education|professional|personal|seasonal] default: "search"`

What to verify that the user can see, per their privacy settings.

Example FBML

Here is example FBML code for `<fb:if-can-see/>`:

```
<fb:if-can-see uid="0123456789" what="photosofme">
  <img src="http://fbmlessentials.staynalive.com/images/me.jpg"
  alt="external image of me" />
  <fb:else> Sorry - you can't see images of me! </fb:else>
</fb:if-can-see>
```

Rendered HTML for Single Instance of Tag

This is the rendered HTML if user 0123456789 can see your photos (based on your privacy settings):

```
<img src="http://fbmlessentials.staynalive.com/images/me.jpg"
     alt="external image of me />
```

(Note that an image would be rendered in the browser.)

This is the rendered HTML if user 0123456789 cannot see your photos:

```
Sorry - you can't see images of me!
```

Additional Information

- This tag supports `<fb:else/>`.
- This tag may be used only on a user's canvas page.

<fb:if-can-see-photo/>

`<fb:if-can-see-photo>...<fb:else>...</fb:else></fb:if-can-see-photo>`

If a user's privacy settings for a particular photo allow you to see the photo, this tag renders the enclosed content. It's great for ensuring that your content appears only to users who can see the photo.

FBML-Specific Attributes

Required

`pid=[int] default: none`
: The ID of the photo, to verify whether the user has permission to see it.

Optional

`uid=[int] default: none`
: The ID of the user whose photo you want to retrieve privacy settings for. This attribute is needed only if you're manually inserting the `pid` and the `pid` is not API-supplied.

Example FBML

Here is example FBML code for `<fb:if-can-see-photo/>`:

```
<fb:if-can-see-photo pid="1988312" uid="683545112">
  <fb:photo pid=" 1988312" uid=" 683545112"/> Display text about
      photo here. <fb:else> Sorry - you can't see that photo,
      and therefore, no description for you! </fb:else>
</fb:if-can-see>
```

Rendered HTML for Single Instance of Tag

If user 683545112 can see the photo with the ID 1988312 (based on your privacy settings), the rendered HTML looks like this:

```
<img pid="1988312" uid="683545112"
     src="http://photos-a.ak.facebook.com/photos-ak-sf2p/v170/243/47/
         683545112/n683545112_1988312_6347.jpg" />
  Display text about photo here.
```

Here is the rendered HTML if user 683545112 cannot see the photo with the ID 1988312:

```
Sorry - you can't see that photo, and therefore, no description for you!
```

Additional Information

- This tag supports `<fb:else/>`.
- This tag may be used only on a user's canvas page.

<fb:if-is-app-user/>

`<fb:if-is-app-user>...<fb:else>...</fb:else></fb:if-is-app-user>`

Renders content within the tags if the user has added the application. Remember, content on canvas pages can be rendered for any user—Facebook member or not—who visits your app. This tag ensures that content renders only for existing Facebook members who have added your application. See also the description of the `<fb:if-user-has-added-app/>` tag later in this chapter.

FBML-Specific Attributes

Required

None.

Optional

`uid=[int] default: loggedinuser`
: The ID of the user. Use `uid` when displaying friends of a user who you want to ensure haven't added the app. This works great for notification invite forms.

Example FBML

Here is example FBML code for `<fb:if-is-app-user/>`:

```
<fb:if-is-app-user> You have the application installed!
  <fb:else> Please install the application! </fb:else>
</fb:if-is-app-user>
```

Rendered HTML for Single Instance of Tag

The following shows up only if the user has installed the application:

```
You have the application installed!
```

The following shows up only if the user has not installed the application:

```
Please install the application!
```

Additional Information

- This tag supports `<fb:else/>`.
- This tag may be used only on a user's canvas page.
- The difference between this tag and `<fb:if-user-has-added-app/>` is that this tag signifies only that the user has accepted the terms and conditions for your app. Use the other tag to ensure that the app has been fully added to a user's account.

<fb:if-is-friends-with-viewer/>

```
<fb:if-is-friends-with-viewer>...<fb:else>...</fb:else>
   </fb:if-is-friends-with-viewer>
```

Renders different content for those who may not be friends with the app user and those who are friends with the app user.

FBML-Specific Attributes

Required

None.

Optional

`uid=[int] default: profileowner`
: The ID of the user you want to verify as a friend of the viewer.

`includeself=[true|false] default: true`
: If the viewer is actually the user with the specified ID and this is `true`, the tag returns `true`.

Example FBML

Here is example FBML code for `<fb:if-is-friends-with-viewer/>`:

```
<fb:if-is-friends-with-viewer> The two of you are friends
  <fb:else> The two of you are not friends </fb:else>
</fb:if-is-app-user>
```

Rendered HTML for Single Instance of Tag

If the current viewer is friends with the person who has installed the application, the rendered HTML looks like this:

```
The two of you are friends
```

If the current viewer is not friends with the person who has installed the application, the rendered HTML looks like this:

```
The two of you are not friends
```

Additional Information

- This tag supports `<fb:else/>`.
- This tag may be used only on a user's canvas page.

<fb:if-is-group-member/>

`<fb:if-is-group-member>...<fb:else>...</fb:else></fb:if-is-group-member>`

Content within this tag renders only if the user is a member of a specified group. This tag can also be used to determine whether a particular user is an admin or an officer in a specified group.

FBML-Specific Attributes

Required

`gid=[int]`
: The group ID used to verify whether a user is part of that group.

Optional

`uid=[int] default: profileowner`
: The ID of the user you want to verify as a member of the group with the specified `gid`.

`role=[member|officer|admin] default: member`
: If you want to verify whether a user actually has a particular role within a group, use something other than `member` here. If `officer` is specified, and a `gid` is specified, the logged-in user must be an officer in the specified group in order for the content to render.

Example FBML

Here is example FBML code for `<fb:is-group-member/>`:

```
<fb:if-is-group-member gid="1234567890"> Congrats! You belong to
      the group specified!
  <fb:else> Sorry - you don't belong to the group specified </fb:else>
</fb:if-is-app-user>
```

Here is a second example:

```
<fb:if-is-group-member gid="1234567890" role="admin"> The logged in
      user is an admin of this group.
  <fb:else> Sorry - you're not an admin of this group! </fb:else>
</fb:if-is-group-member>
```

Rendered HTML for Single Instance of Tag

For the first example, if the current user is part of the group with an ID of 1234567890, the rendered HTML looks like this:

```
Congrats! You belong to the group specified!
```

For the first example, if the current user is not part of the group with an ID of 1234567890, the rendered HTML looks like this:

```
Sorry - you don't belong to the group specified
```

For the second example, if the current user is an admin of the group with an ID of 1234567890, the rendered HTML looks like this:

```
The logged in user is an admin of this group.
```

For the second example, if the current user is not an admin of the group with an ID of 1234567890, the rendered HTML looks like this:

```
Sorry - you're not an admin of this group!
```

Additional Information

- This tag supports `<fb:else/>`.
- This tag may be used only on a user's canvas page.

<fb:if-is-user/>

```
<fb:if-is-user>...<fb:else>...</fb:else></fb:if-is-user>
```

Within this tag, specify the IDs of the users for whom you would like to render content. Only the users with listed IDs will be able to see that content.

FBML-Specific Attributes

Required

`uid=[int] default: none`
: The ID of the user for whom to display content. For multiple users, separate multiple user IDs with commas.

Optional

None.

Example FBML

Here is example FBML code for `<fb:if-is-user/>`:

```
<fb:if-is-user uid="1234567890,0987654321"> You're special
  <fb:else> Sorry - you're one of the unprivileged. </fb:else>
</fb:if-is-user>
```

Rendered HTML for Single Instance of Tag

If you're the user with the ID 1234567890 or 0987654321, the rendered HTML looks like this:

```
You're special
```

If you're not one of the two listed users, the rendered HTML looks like this:

```
Sorry - you're one of the unprivileged.
```

Additional Information

- This tag supports `<fb:else/>`.

- This tag may be used only on a user's canvas page.

<fb:if-user-has-added-app/>

```
<fb:if-user-has-added-app>...<fb:else>...</fb:else>
    </fb:if-user-has-added-app>
```

Content between the tags is rendered only if the user has completely added the application to their Facebook account. See also the description of the `<fb:if-is-app-user/>` tag earlier in this chapter.

FBML-Specific Attributes

Required

None.

Optional

`uid=[int] default: loggedinuser`
: The user ID used to verify whether the listed user has added the app.

Example FBML

Here is example FBML code for `<fb:if-user-has-added-app/>`:

```
<fb:if-user-has-added-app uid="1234567890"> Thanks for adding the app!
  <fb:else> Please add the app.  </fb:else>
</fb:if-user-has-added-app>
```

Rendered HTML for Single Instance of Tag

If the user with the ID 1234567890 has added the app, the rendered HTML looks like this:

```
Thanks for adding the app!
```

If the user with the ID 1234567890 has not added the app, the rendered HTML looks like this:

```
Please add the app.
```

Additional Information

- This tag supports `<fb:else/>`.
- This tag may be used only on a user's canvas page.
- The difference between this tag and the `<fb:if-is-app-user/>` tag is that the latter only requires the user to agree to the terms and conditions of the app for the tag to return the content within, whereas this tag returns content only if the user has completely added the app.

Profile and Facebook Page Authorization Tags

The user's profile is the most visited part of any application. It is the landing page for any search related to that user, and as such, it handles traffic for all apps installed by that user. Therefore, you can see why it is important to develop a good strategy for incorporating the profile into your application. This is especially true for Facebook's new profile design (to be launched soon after this book goes to press), which adds even more ways you can adapt your application into a user profile.* Successfully incorporating the profile into your application is one of many methods you can use to increase installs for your application.

It's important to note that all of the profile and Facebook Page authorization tags listed in this section are not compatible with the `<fb:else/>` tag. They are also not compatible with Facebook canvas pages.

<fb:visible-to-owner/>

`<fb:visible-to-owner>...</fb:visible-to-owner>`

Renders the content within the tags only to the owner of a profile or the admin of a page. The content is hidden, but it's still viewable in the source HTML. This tag may be used only on a user's profile.

FBML-Specific Attributes

Required

None.

Optional

`bgcolor=[color] default: none`
: The background color in which the text rendered in the box will appear.

Example FBML

Here is example FBML code for `<fb:visible-to-owner/>`:

```
<fb:visible-to-owner> Welcome to your app! </fb:visible-to-owner>
```

Rendered HTML for Single Instance of Tag

If you visit the app you have installed, the rendered HTML looks like this:

```
Welcome to your app!
```

* Please visit this book's Facebook Page at *http://page.fbmlessentials.com* for updates on how to do this when the new design is released.

Additional Information

- Be careful not to use this tag to render sensitive information. The content rendered by this tag, whether shown in the browser or not, is always available in the source on the page.
- This tag works only on a user's profile.
- Tags that control title, subtitle, and noninline tags will not render within this tag.

<fb:visible-to-user/>

`<fb:visible-to-user>...</fb:visible-to-user>`

Displays the content within the tags only to the profile owner and the specified user. If this tag is used on a Facebook Page, the content renders to a specified fan as well as to the admin of the page.

FBML-Specific Attributes

Required

`uid=[`*`int`*`] default: none`
: The ID of the user for whom you would like to display content. Note that this *cannot* be a comma-separated list (as the `<fb:if-is-user/>` tag can use) for canvas pages.

Optional

`bgcolor=[color] default: none`
: The background color in which the text rendered in the box will appear.

Example FBML

Here is example FBML code for `<fb:if-is-user/>`:

```
<fb:visible-to-user uid="0123456789"> You are user 0123456789.
    </fb:visible-to-owner>
```

Rendered HTML for Single Instance of Tag

If you visit the app and you are either the user with the ID 0123456789 or the owner of the app, the rendered HTML looks like this:

```
You are user 0123456789.
```

Additional Information

- Be careful not to use this tag to render sensitive information. The content rendered by this tag, whether shown in the browser or not, is always available in the source on the page.
- This tag works only on a user's profile.

<fb:visible-to-friends/>

`<fb:visible-to-friends>...</fb:visible-to-friends>`

Renders the content within the tags only to the user who has installed the application and to that user's friends. This tag does not work on Facebook Pages.

FBML-Specific Attributes

Required

None.

Optional

`bgcolor=[color] default: none`
: The background color in which the text rendered in the box will appear.

Example FBML

Here is example FBML for `<fb:visible-to-friends/>`:

```
<fb:visible-to-friends> Greetings, friend!
              </fb:visible-to-friends>
```

Rendered HTML for Single Instance of Tag

If your friend visits your profile, or if you visit your own profile, the rendered HTML looks like this:

```
Greetings, friend!
```

Additional Information

- Be careful not to use this tag to render sensitive information. The content rendered by this tag, whether shown in the browser or not, is always available in the source on the page.
- This tag works only on a user's profile.
- Use the `<fb:visible-to-connection/>` tag (described later in this chapter) if you want to verify fans of a Page as well as friends of a user.

<fb:visible-to-app-users/>

```
<fb:visible-to-app-users>...</fb:visible-to-app-users>
```

Renders the content between the tags only if the user has been granted full access to use the app (i.e., they have agreed to the terms and conditions). However, the user does not necessarily have to have fully added the app in order to see the content. Use `<fb:visible-to-added-app-users/>` (described later in this chapter) to verify that the user has completely added the app to their account.

FBML-Specific Attributes

Required

None.

Optional

`bgcolor=[color] default: none`
: The background color in which the text rendered in the box will appear.

Example FBML

Here is example FBML code for `<fb:visible-to-app-users/>`:

```
<fb:visible-to-app-users> Welcome to the club!
    </fb:visible-to-app-users>
```

Rendered HTML for Single Instance of Tag

If a user who has been granted access to use the app visits your profile, the rendered HTML looks like this:

```
Welcome to the club!
```

Additional Information

- Be careful not to use this tag to render sensitive information. The content rendered by this tag, whether shown in the browser or not, is always available in the source on the page.
- This tag works only on a user's profile.

<fb:visible-to-added-app-users/>

```
<fb:visible-to-added-app-users>...</fb:visible-to-added-app-users>
```

Renders the content between the tags only if the user has completely added the app to their account.

FBML-Specific Attributes

Required

None.

Optional

`bgcolor=[color] default: none`
: The background color in which the text rendered in the box will appear.

Example FBML

Here is example FBML code for `<fb:visible-to-added-app-users/>`:

```
<fb:visible-to-added-app-users> Welcome to the club!
          </fb:visible-to-added-app-users>
```

Rendered HTML for Single Instance of Tag

If a user who has completely added the app to their account visits your profile, the rendered HTML looks like this:

```
Welcome to the club!
```

Additional Information

- Be careful not to use this tag to render sensitive information. The content rendered by this tag, whether shown in the browser or not, is always available in the source on the page.
- This tag works only on a user's profile.
- Use `<fb:visible-to-app-users/>` (described earlier) if you care only whether a user has agreed to your app's terms and conditions, not necessarily whether they have added the app to their account.

<fb:visible-to-connection/>

`<fb:visible-to-connection>...</fb:visible-to-connection>`

Displays the content within the tags only if the user is a friend of the user whose profile they are visiting, or is a fan of the Facebook Page they are visiting. The content also renders for the profile owner and the Page admin.

FBML-Specific Attributes

Required

None.

Optional

`bgcolor=[color] default: none`
: The background color in which the text rendered in the box will appear.

Example FBML

Here is example FBML code for `<fb:visible-to-connection/>`:

```
<fb:visible-to-connection> Thank you to my fans!
    </fb:visible-to-connection>
```

Rendered HTML for Single Instance of Tag

If the user is one of your Facebook friends or is a fan of the Page you are an admin of, or if you visit the profile or Page yourself, the rendered HTML looks like this:

```
Thank you to my fans!
```

Additional Information

- Be careful not to use this tag to render sensitive information. The content rendered by this tag, whether shown in the browser or not, is always available in the source on the page.
- This tag works only on a user's profile.
- See the description of `<fb:visible-to-friends/>` earlier in this chapter for another example. Note, however, that the `<fb:visible-to-friends/>` tag is much more limited, so it is recommended that you use the `<fb:visible-to-connection/>` tag.

Logic Tags

Two types of logic tags exist in FBML: 1) the `<fb:if/>` and `<fb:else/>` tags, and 2) the `<fb:switch/>` tag. Each type renders data based on a set of criteria being true or false. Of course, with any logic tag, a condition is required. If the condition is satisfied, content is rendered. If the condition is not satisfied, subsequent conditions are evaluated, or else content is not rendered.

<fb:if/>

```
<fb:if>...<fb:else>...</fb:else></fb:if>
```

Renders the content within the tags only if the value is equal to `true`. If the value is set to `false`, nothing is returned. For this tag to be useful, some external programming is necessary to set the content of the value either to `true` or `false`.

FBML-Specific Attributes

Required

None.

Optional

`value=[true|false] default: false`
    Returns the content within the tags unless `value="false"`.

Example FBML

Here is example FBML code for `<fb:if/>`:

```
<fb:if value="true"> Display some content here </fb:if>
```

Rendered HTML for Single Instance of Tag

If the `value` attribute is set to `true`, the rendered HTML looks like this:

```
Display some content here
```

<fb:else/>

`<fb:else>...</fb:else>`

Renders the content within the tags only if the condition specified in the containing tags is `false`. It is compatible within any type of `<fb:if*/>` tag or the `<fb:is-in-network/>` tag, as well as within the `<fb:is-it-april-fools/>`, `<fb:is-it-christmas/>`, `<fb:18-plus/>`, and `<fb:21-plus/>` tags.

FBML-Specific Attributes

Required

None.

Optional

None.

Example FBML

Here is example FBML code for `<fb:else/>`:

```
<fb:if value="true"> Display content here only if value="true".
    <fb:else> If fb:if's value were "false", then this would
    be displayed. </fb:else> </fb:if>
```

Here is a second example:

```
<fb:if-is-user uid="1,2,3"> Display content here only if the
    user has id 1,2,3. <fb:else> If uid is 4, 10, or anything
    but 1,2,3, display this content. </fb:else> </fb:if>
```

Rendered HTML for Single Instance of Tag

In the first example, because `value="true"`, the rendered HTML will always look like this:

```
Display content here only if value="true".
```

In the second example, if the user ID is 1, 2, or 3, the rendered HTML will look like this:

```
Display content here only if the user has id 1,2,3.
```

In the second example, if the user ID is not 1, 2, or 3, the rendered HTML will look like this:

```
If uid is 4, 10, or anything but 1,2,3, display this content.
```

Additional Information

- `<fb:else/>` is compatible within the following tags:

```
<fb:if/>
<fb:if-can-see/>
<fb:if-can-see-photo/>
<fb:if-is-app-user/>
<fb:if-is-friends-with-viewer/>
<fb:if-is-group-member/>
<fb:if-is-own-profile/>
<fb:if-is-user/>
<fb:if-user-has-added-app/>
<fb:is-in-network/>
<fb:is-it-christmas/>
<fb:is-it-april-fools/>
```

<fb:switch/>

```
<fb:switch>...<fb:default>...</fb:default></fb:switch>
```

Reads each tag within the tags, and the first one that returns content other than an empty string gets returned as output.

FBML-Specific Attributes

Required

None.

Optional

None.

Example FBML

Here is example FBML code for `<fb:switch/>`:

```
<fb:switch> <fb:name uid="3"/> <!-- if name is blank, move
    on --> <fb:is-it-christmas> It's Christmas! </fb:is-it-christmas>
    <!-- if it's not christmas, move on --> <fb:default> If all the
    above tags return nothing, display this text </fb:default>
</fb:switch>
```

Rendered HTML for Single Instance of Tag

If `<fb:name/>` returns a name, the rendered HTML looks like this:

```
Rendered name for user with id '3' ('Jesse Stay')
```

If `<fb:name/>` returns nothing, but it's Christmas day, the rendered HTML looks like this:

```
It's Christmas!
```

If both `<fb:name/>` and `<fb:is-it-christmas/>` return nothing, the rendered HTML looks like this:

```
If all the above tags return nothing, display this text
```

<fb:default/>

`<fb:default>...</fb:default>`

Always returns the content within. Used as the last tag within an `<fb:switch/>` tag, this tag guarantees that if all tags within don't return anything, at least the content within will be returned.

FBML-Specific Attributes

Required

None.

Optional

None.

Example FBML

See the example under the `<fb:switch/>` tag earlier in this chapter.

Additional Information

- Again, `<fb:default/>` *always* returns the content within. Therefore, to be useful, it must always be the last tag in an `<fb:switch/>` statement.

Random Logic

Of course, for a completely random selection of content to display, the `<fb:random/>` tag is your friend.

<fb:random/>

`<fb:random>...<fb:random-option>...</fb:random-option></fb:random>`

Allows you to specify a set of individual pieces of content. Facebook will then randomly pick—based on the weight you specify—one or more of the options you chose. `<fb:random/>` is especially useful in user profiles, where data cannot be explicitly dynamic.

FBML-Specific Attributes

Required

None.

Optional

`pick=[`*`int`*`] default: 1`
: Specifies the number of `<fb:random-option/>`s to return.

`unique=[true|false] default: true`
: If `pick` is greater than 1, specifies whether to enforce the returned values to be unique.

Example FBML

Here is example FBML code for `<fb:random/>`:

```
<fb:random> <fb:random-option> randomly selected text 1
    </fb:random-option> <fb:random-option> randomly selected
    text 2 </fb:random-option>
</fb:random>
```

Rendered HTML for Single Instance of Tag

The HTML for the example just shown renders randomly. It will either look like this:

```
randomly selected text 1
```

Or like this:

```
randomly selected text 2 will be displayed.
```

<fb:random-option/>

```
<fb:random-option>...</fb:random-option>
```

Compatible with only the `<fb:random/>` tag, this tag specifies an item within `<fb:random/>` that is to be randomly selected and returned to the browser.

FBML-Specific Attributes

Required

None.

Optional

`weight=[`*`float`*`] default: 1.0`
: Helps control the frequency of the specified item.

Example FBML

Here is example FBML code for `<fb:random-option/>` (see the example under the `<fb:random/>` tag earlier for context):

```
<fb:random-option weight="2"> This text appears twice as
    often as one with a weight of 1 </fb:random-option>
```

Messaging and Alerts in FBML

FBML provides some very useful tags for displaying both messages and errors to your application's users. These tags will display a standard Facebook error or message, using Facebook's style guidelines. It is strongly recommended that you use these tags for errors and messages because they keep the Facebook look and feel consistent within your application. This section is a list of tags that will render standard Facebook errors and messages. I'll provide examples and images for each tag so you can see what they look like in real life.

<fb:error/>

```
<fb:error>...[<fb:message>...</fb:message>]</fb:error>
```

Renders a standard Facebook error message. This message appears in a standard pink box.

FBML-Specific Attributes

Required

`message=[string] default: none`
: The error message heading to display in the error box. Optionally, you can use an `<fb:message/>` internally to specify the error heading.

Optional

`decoration=[no_padding|shorten] default: none`
: Modifies the appearance of the error box. `no_padding` removes the 20 pixels of padding that surrounds the error box, and `shorten` removes the 20 pixels of padding below the error message.

Example FBML*

Here is example FBML code for `<fb:error/>` by itself (using the `message` attribute):

```
<fb:error message="Don't touch that button!"/>
```

Here is example FBML code for `<fb:error/>` with an `<fb:message/>` tag embedded:

```
<fb:error> Don't touch that button! <fb:message> Danger, Will Robinson!
    </fb:message> </fb:error>
```

Rendered HTML for Single Instance of Tag

The rendered HTML for the first example looks like this (Figure 3-2 shows the result):

```
<div class="standard_message has_padding"><h1 id="error"> Don&#039;t
    touch that button!</h1></div>
```

Don't touch that button!

Figure 3-2. The <fb:error/> tag by itself

The rendered HTML for the second example looks like this (Figure 3-3 shows the result):

```
<div class="standard_message has_padding"><h1 id="error"> Danger,
    Will Robinson! <p> Don't touch that button! </p> </h1></div>
```

* See this example in action at *http://apps.facebook.com/fbmlessentials/?action=error*.

Danger, Will Robinson!
Don't touch that button!

Figure 3-3. The <fb:error/> tag when used with <fb:message/>

Additional Information

- The `<fb:error/>` tag must contain one `<fb:message/>` tag or one `message` attribute to specify the error heading text.
- The content for the error is optional.

<fb:explanation/>

```
<fb:explanation>...[<fb:message>...</fb:message>]</fb:explanation>
```

Renders a standard Facebook explanation message. This message appears in a standard gray box.

FBML-Specific Attributes

Required

`message=[string] default: none`
: The explanation message heading to display in the explanation box. Optionally, you can use an `<fb:message/>` internally to specify the explanation heading.

Optional

`decoration=[no_padding|shorten] default: none`
: Modifies the appearance of the explanation box. `no_padding` removes the 20 pixels of padding that surrounds the explanation box, and `shorten` removes the 20 pixels of padding below the explanation message.

Example FBML*

Here is example FBML code for `<fb:explanation/>` by itself (using the `message` attribute):

```
<fb:explanation message="This is why you shouldn't have pushed the button."/>
```

And here is example FBML code for `<fb:explanation/>` with an `<fb:message/>` tag embedded:

* You can see this example in action at *http://apps.facebook.com/fbmlessentials/?action=explanation*.

```
<fb:explanation> This is why you shouldn't have pushed the button.
    <fb:message> We told you! </fb:message> </fb:explanation>
```

Rendered HTML for Single Instance of Tag

The rendered HTML for the first example looks like this (Figure 3-4 shows the result):

```
<div class="standard_message has_padding"><h1 class="explanation_note">
    This is why you shouldn&#039;t have pushed the button. </h1></div>
```

This is why you shouldn't have pushed the button.

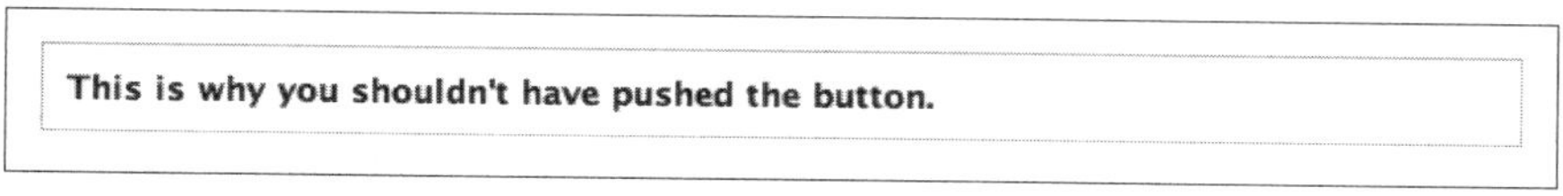

Figure 3-4. The <fb:explanation/> tag by itself

The rendered HTML for the second example looks like this (Figure 3-5 shows the result):

```
<div class="standard_message has_padding"><h1 class="explanation_note">
    We told you! <p> This is why you shouldn't have pushed the button.
    </p> </h1></div>
```

We told you!

This is why you shouldn't have pushed the button.

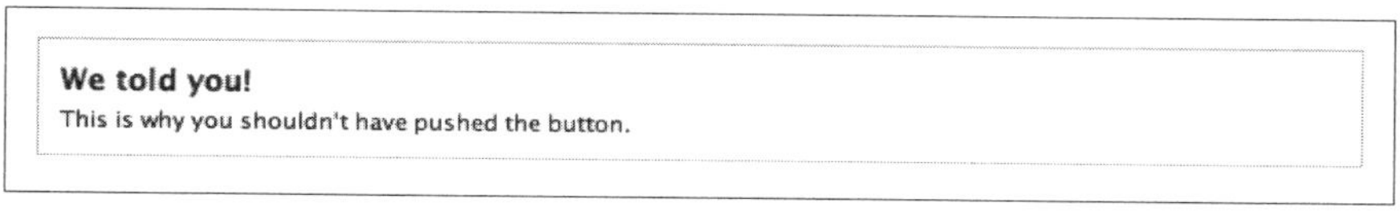

Figure 3-5. The <fb:explanation/> tag when used with <fb:message/>

Additional Information

- The `<fb:explanation/>` tag must contain one `<fb:message/>` tag or one `message` attribute to specify the explanation heading text.
- The content for the explanation is optional.

<fb:success/>

```
<fb:success>...[<fb:message>...</fb:message>]</fb:success>
```

Renders a standard Facebook success message. This message appears in a standard pink box.

FBML-Specific Attributes

Required

`message=[`*`string`*`] default: none`
: The explanation message heading to display in the success box. Optionally, you can use an `<fb:message/>` internally to specify the success heading.

Optional

`decoration=[no_padding|shorten] default: none`
: Modifies the appearance of the success box. `no_padding` removes the 20 pixels of padding that surrounds the success box, and `shorten` removes the 20 pixels of padding below the success message.

Example FBML*

Here is example FBML code for `<fb:success/>` by itself (using the `message` attribute):

```
<fb:success message="Congratulations! You pressed the green button."/>
```

And here is example FBML code for `<fb:success/>` with an `<fb:message/>` tag embedded:

```
<fb:success> Congratulations! You pressed the green button.
    <fb:message> Congratulations! </fb:message> </fb:success>
```

Rendered HTML for Single Instance of Tag

The rendered HTML for the first example looks like this (Figure 3-6 shows the resulting success message):

```
<div class="standard_message has_padding"><h1 class="status">
    Congratulations! You pressed the green button. </h1></div>
```

Congratulations! You pressed the green button.

Figure 3-6. The <fb:success/> tag by itself

The rendered HTML for the second example looks like this (Figure 3-7 shows the resulting success message):

```
<div class="standard_message has_padding"><h1 class="status">
    Congratulations! <p> Congratulations! You pressed the
    green button. </p> </h1></div>
```

* You can see this example in action at *http://apps.facebook.com/fbmlessentials/?action=success*.

Congratulations!
Congratulations! You pressed the green button.

Figure 3-7. The <fb:success/> tag when used with <fb:message/>

Additional Information

- The `<fb:success/>` tag must contain one `<fb:message/>` tag or one `message` attribute to specify the success heading text.
- The content for the explanation is optional.

Profile-Specific Tags

To set profile-specific tags, or to render anything in a user's profile for the application, you must either place the code in your "Default FBML" box in your application settings or make an explicit `profile.setFBML` call via the API. It's important to understand that FBML on a user's profile is not dynamic. This means that if you change the FBML, you must either set it through the "Default FBML" box in your application settings or make an API call via `profile.setFBML` again to reset the FBML for that user's profile. Just refreshing the user's profile page *will not* refresh it with your new FBML! The following tags work only in the application's profile box on a user's profile.

<fb:wide/>

```
<fb:wide>...</fb:wide>
```

FBML placed between these tags displays only when the application's profile box is in the wide column on a user's profile. See the description of the `<fb:narrow/>` tag next for how to display in the narrow column. In your application settings, I strongly suggest that you set the default column for your application to narrow. This is because most application developers set the default column to wide (as that is the default). However, it is important to set how the application will look in the wide column on a user's profile using the `<fb:wide/>` tag.

FBML-Specific Attributes

Required

None.

Optional

None.

Example FBML

Here is example FBML code for the `<fb:wide/>` tag; add this to your "Default FBML" box in your application settings (or you can set it via the `setFBML` API call):

```
<fb:wide>
  When a user drags the application profile box into the wide column
  on their profile, this code will appear.
</fb:wide>
```

Rendered HTML for Single Instance of Tag

In our FBML Essentials application, when dragging the profile to the wide column of your profile (after adding the app), it will look like Figure 3-8.

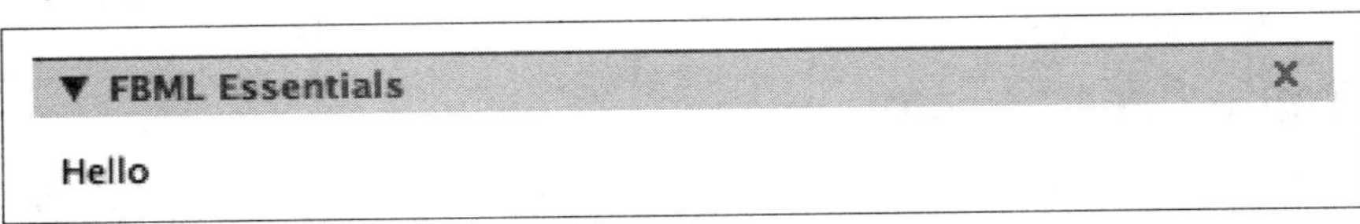

Figure 3-8. The application profile box in the wide column of a user's profile

Additional Information

- Code within the `<fb:wide/>` tags renders in a 388-pixel-wide box on the user's profile (not including margins). There is also an 8-pixel left margin, and no right margin. To center your content, make your content 380 pixels wide.
- Code not placed in `<fb:narrow/>` or `<fb:wide/>` tags will show in either column.

<fb:narrow/>

`<fb:narrow>...</fb:narrow>`

FBML placed between these tags displays only when the application's profile box is in the narrow column on a user's profile. See the description of the `<fb:wide/>` tag previously for how to display in the wide column. In the case where you set the default FBML for your application to wide, you will need to set this in the event that your users move the application profile box to the narrow column.

FBML-Specific Attributes

Required

None.

Optional

None.

Example FBML

Here is example FBML code for the `<fb:narrow/>` tag; add this to your "Default FBML" box in your application settings (or you can set it via the `setFBML` API call):

```
<fb:narrow>
  When a user drags the application profile box into the narrow column
      on their profile, this code will appear.
</fb:narrow>
```

Rendered HTML for Single Instance of Tag

In our FBML Essentials application, when dragging the profile to the narrow column of your profile (after adding the app), it will look like Figure 3-9.

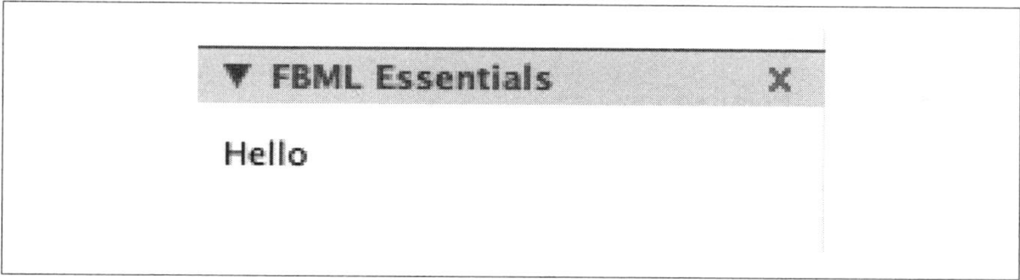

Figure 3-9. The application profile box in the narrow column of a user's profile

Additional Information

- Code within the `<fb:narrow/>` tags renders in a 190-pixel-wide box on the user's profile (not including margins). There is also an 10-pixel right margin, and no left margin. To center your content, make your content 180 pixels wide.
- Code not placed in `<fb:narrow/>` or `<fb:wide/>` tags will show in either column.

<fb:user-table/>

`<fb:user-table><fb:user-item/><fb:user-item/>...</fb:user-table>`

Renders a list of users, specified as `<fb:user-item/>` tags within the tags. Each `<fb:user-item/>` tag renders a thumbnail for the specified user, with a linked name for that user appearing to the right of the thumbnail. Look at the Mutual Friends section on each profile page for a good example of what this looks like.

FBML-Specific Attributes

Required

None.

Optional

`cols=[int]` defaults: 3 *(for narrow column)*, 6 *(for wide column)*
The number of columns in the user table.

Example FBML

The `<fb:user-table/>` tag simply contains a list of `<fb:user-item/>` tags, as shown in the following example (see the `<fb:user-item/>` tag described next for more details):

```
<fb:user-table>
  <fb:user-item uid="683545112"/>
  <fb:user-item uid="4"/>
  <fb:user-item uid="7403766"/>
</fb:user-table>
```

Rendered HTML for Single Instance of Tag

When rendered, an `<fb:user-table/>` box on a user's profile will produce HTML that looks like this (Figure 3-10 shows the result):

```
<table class="friendTable" cellpadding="0" cellspacing="0" border="0"
    height="100%">
<tr>
<td >
  <table height="100%">
  <tr>
    <td height="100%" style="vertical-align: middle;">
      <a href="http://www.facebook.com/profile.php?id=683545112">
          <img src="http://profile.ak.facebook.com/profile5/623/6/
              t683545112_5427.jpg"
          alt=""  class="" /></a>
    </td>
  </tr>
  <tr>
    <td>
      <a href="http://www.facebook.com/profile.php?id=683545112">
          Jesse Stay</a>
    </td>
  </tr>
  </table>
</td>
<td >
  <table height="100%">
  <tr>
    <td height="100%" style="vertical-align: middle;">
      <a href="http://www.facebook.com/s.php?k=100000080&id=4">
          <img src="http://profile.ak.facebook.com/profile5/1240/77/
              t4_65.jpg"
          alt=""  class="" /></a>
    </td>
  </tr>
  <tr>
```

```
      <td>
        <a href="http://www.facebook.com/s.php?k=100000080&id=4">
            Mark Zuckerberg</a>
      </td>
    </tr>
    </table>
  </td>
  <td >
    <table height="100%">
    <tr>
      <td height="100%" style="vertical-align: middle;">
        <a href="http://www.facebook.com/profile.php?id=7403766">
            <img src="http://profile.ak.facebook.com/profile5/1161/15/
                t7403766_2745.jpg"
            alt=""  class="" /></a>
      </td>
    </tr>
    <tr>
      <td>
        <a href="http://www.facebook.com/profile.php?id=7403766">
            Nick ONeill</a>
      </td>
    </tr>
    </table>
  </td>
  <td >
    <table height="100%"></table>
  </td>
  <td >
    <table height="100%"></table>
  </td>
  <td >
    <table height="100%"></table>
  </td>
  </tr>
  </table>
```

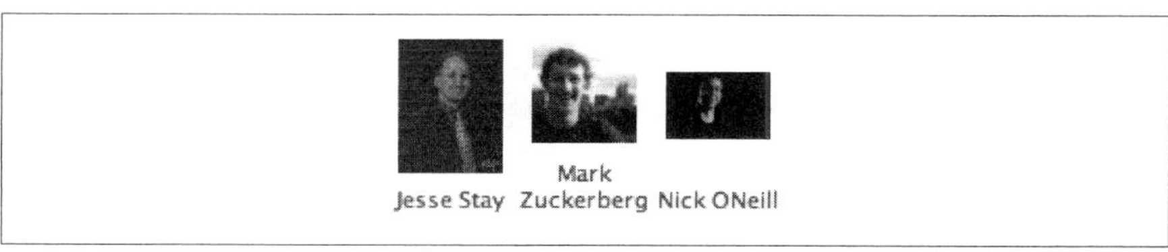

Figure 3-10. The result of our <fb:user-table/> example

Additional Information

- As with all tags in this section, `<fb:user-table/>` can be used only a user's profile, nowhere else.

<fb:user-item/>

```
<fb:user-item uid="..."/>
```

To be used within `<fb:user-table/>`, this tag renders a thumbnail image and name to the right of that image that links to that user's profile. See the earlier description of the `<fb:user-table/>` tag for context.

FBML-Specific Attributes

Required

`uid=[bigint] default: none`
: The user ID of the user item to render.

Optional

None.

Example FBML

Here is an example of the `<fb:user-item/>` tag (see `<fb:user-table/>` for context):

```
<fb:user-item uid="683545112"/>
```

Rendered HTML for Single Instance of Tag

The underlying HTML looks like this (Figure 3-11 shows the result):

```
<table height="100%">
  <tr>
    <td height="100%" style="vertical-align: middle;">
      <a href="http://www.facebook.com/profile.php?id=683545112">
          <img src="http://profile.ak.facebook.com/profile5/623/6/
              t683545112_5427.jpg"
          alt=""  class="" /></a>
    </td>
  </tr>
  <tr>
    <td>
      <a href="http://www.facebook.com/profile.php?id=683545112">
          Jesse Stay</a>
    </td>
  </tr>
</table>
```

Figure 3-11. A single <fb:user-item/> instance

<fb:subtitle/>

`<fb:subtitle>...</fb:subtitle>`

Renders a subtitle box below the title of your app in the user's profile. With `<fb:action/>` tags, this tag will render several links on the righthand side.

FBML-Specific Attributes

Required

None.

Optional

`seeallurl=[`*`string`*`]`
: Renders a "see all" link, with a specified URL. The URL must be a canvas page URL (i.e., *http://apps.facebook.com/...*).

Example FBML

Here is example FBML code for `<fb:subtitle/>`. It renders a subtitle box below the title on the app's profile box on a user's profile (Figure 3-12 shows the result—visit the FBML Essentials app to see it in action!):

```
<fb:subtitle>
  by Jesse Stay, published by O'Reilly
  <fb:action href="http://apps.facebook.com/oreilly"> Purchase the Book!
      </fb:action>
</fb:subtitle>
```

Figure 3-12. The result of our <fb:subtitle/> example

Additional Information

- This tag does not work with `<fb:visible-*/>` tags.
- This tag can have multiple `<fb:action/>` tags within it.

Users, Groups, Events, Networks, and Applications

<fb:name/>

```
<fb:name uid="..."/>
```

Renders the name of the specified user. With various attributes you can customize how that name is displayed.

FBML-Specific Attributes

Required

`uid=[`*`string`*`|loggedinuser|profileowner]`
: The ID of the user whose name you would like to display. **`loggedinuser`** displays the name of the user viewing the profile, whereas **`profileowner`** can be used to display the name of the owner of the profile being viewed.

Optional

`firstnameonly=[true|false] default: false`
: If `true`, displays just the first name of the user.

`linked=[true|false] default: true`
: If `true`, links the name to the listed user's profile.

`lastnameonly=[true|false] default: true`
: If `true`, displays just the last name of the user.

`possessive=[true|false] default: false`
: If `true`, makes the name possessive (adds *'s* to the name, turning *Jesse* into *Jesse's*).

`reflexive=[true|false] default: false`
: If `true`, and `useyou` is `true`, turns the pronoun "you" into "yourself."

`shownetwork=[true|false] default: false`
: If `true`, and an actual Facebook ID other than `profileowner` or `loggedinuser` is used, the name will display the user's network in parentheses to the right of the name (see the example for this tag).

`useyou=[true|false] default: true`
: If `true`, and the profile owner is the same as the logged-in user, displays "you" as the user's name.

`ifcantsee=[`*`string`*`] default:` *`empty string`*
: Specifies text to display in case a user viewing the current user's profile or canvas page doesn't have permission to see the user's name.

`capitalize=[true|false] default: false`
: If `useyou` is `true` and the specified `uid` is the logged-in user, capitalizes "YOU".

`subjectid=[`*`string`*`] default: none`
: The user ID of the subject of the sentence when the name is the object of the verb of the sentence. Use this tag when there are two `<fb:name/>` tags in a sentence and you want to make sure the sentence that's displayed is grammatically correct when you're visiting your own profile, when the subject is visiting your profile, or when the subject is visiting his own profile. (The example for this tag shows this in action.)

Example FBML

Here is example FBML code for `<fb:name/>`, using `shownetwork="true"` and `subjectid="683545112"`:

```
<fb:name uid="683545112"/> wrote about <fb:name uid="4"
    shownetwork="true" subjectid="683545112"/>!
```

Rendered HTML for Single Instance of Tag

The underlying HTML for the example looks like this (Figure 3-13 shows the result):

```
you wrote about
 <a href="http://www.facebook.com/s.php?k=100000080&id=4"
     onclick="(new Image()).src = '/ajax/ct.php?app_id=4556145827&action_
     type=3&post_form_id=d05d40629636f8c5af8da6b3c997e549&position=2&' +
     Math.random();return true;">Mark Zuckerberg</a> (Facebook)!
```

you wrote about Mark Zuckerberg (Facebook)!

Figure 3-13. The result of our <fb:name/> example, when I visit my own profile (my ID is 683545112)

<fb:pronoun/>

```
<fb:pronoun uid="..."/>
```

Renders a pronoun for the specified user.

FBML-Specific Attributes

Required

`uid=[string|actor]`
: The ID of the user to render a pronoun for. Use `actor` when using this tag in a feed story to help render a pronoun for the actor.

A *feed story* is a blurb of text about the user of your app. This blurb gets put in the user's Mini-Feed, where it has the potential to be sent to all of the user's friends. See the section on "Feed Forms" later in this chapter to learn how you can use plain FBML/HTML to send a feed story to the Mini-Feed of a user (i.e., the actor).

Optional

`useyou=[true|false] default: true`
: Renders the pronoun "you" if you are the specified `uid` visiting the profile or canvas page.

`possessive=[true|false] default: false`
: Renders a possessive form of the user (his/her/your/their).

`reflexive=[true|false] default: false`
: Renders a reflexive form of the user (himself/herself/yourself/themself).

`objective=[true|false] default: false`
: Renders an objective form of the user (him/her/you/them).

`usethey=[true|false] default: true`
: Renders "they" if the user has not specified a gender.

`capitalize=[true|false] default: false`
: Capitalizes the first letter of the pronoun.

Example FBML

The following example FBML code for `<fb:pronoun/>` capitalizes the first letter, renders "they" if the user has not specified a gender, and renders the possessive form of the pronoun (Figure 3-14 shows the result):

```
<fb:name useyou="false" uid="profileowner"/> has just finished
    <fb:pronoun uid="profileowner" possessive="true"
    capitalize="true"/> Book!
```

Jesse Stay has just finished His Book!

Figure 3-14. The result of our first <fb:pronoun/> example

Here is another example (Figure 3-15 shows the result):

```
<fb:name useyou="false" uid="683545112"/> just gave
    <fb:pronoun uid="actor" possessive="true"/> book to Fred.
```

Jesse Stay just gave his book to Fred.

Figure 3-15. The result of our second <fb:pronoun/> example

<fb:profile-pic/>

`<fb:profile-pic uid="..."/>`

Renders the user's profile picture, which is selected in the user's settings.

FBML-Specific Attributes

Required

`uid=[`*`string`*`] default: none`
: The ID of the user to return a profile picture for.

Optional

`size=[thumb|small|normal|square|t|s|n|q] default: thumb`
: The size of the profile picture to render. Options are: `thumb (t)` (50 pixels wide); `small (s)` (100 pixels wide); `normal (n)` (200 pixels wide); or `square (q)` (50 × 50 pixels). The shortcut versions can also be used.

`linked=[true|false] default: true`
: Produces a link for the profile picture back to the user's profile.

Example FBML

The following is example FBML code for a square profile picture using `<fb:profile-pic/>`. Note that any of the possible sizes can be replaced with `square`. This profile picture will also link back to the user's profile:

```
<fb:profile-pic uid="4" size="square"/>
```

Rendered HTML for Single Instance of Tag

The underlying HTML for the profile picture looks like this (Figure 3-16 shows the result):

```
<a href="http://www.facebook.com/s.php?k=100000080&id=4"
    onclick="(new Image()).src = '/ajax/ct.php?app_id=4556145827&action_
    type=3&post_form_id=47574ff04e8cb37298e9ddcc2e84e84c&position=2&'
    + Math.random();return true;">
<img uid="4" size="square" src="http://profile.ak.facebook.com/profile5/
```

```
        1240/77/q4_65.jpg" alt="Mark Zuckerberg" title="Mark Zuckerberg" />
    </a>
```

Figure 3-16. The result of our <fb:profile-pic/> example

Additional Information

- The `<fb:profile-pic/>` is treated like a normal `<img/>` tag.
- All attributes supported by a normal HTML `<img/>` tag should work with the `<fb:profile-pic/>` tag as well.

<fb:eventlink/>

`<fb:eventlink eid="..."/>`

Renders a link to a specified event.

FBML-Specific Attributes

Required

`eid=[`*`int`*`] default: none`
: The ID of the event to link to.

Optional

None.

Example FBML

Here is example FBML code for `<fb:eventlink/>`:

```
<fb:eventlink eid="11436588798"/>
```

Rendered HTML for Single Instance of Tag

The underlying HTML for the example looks like this (Figure 3-17 shows the result):

```
<a href="http://www.facebook.com/event.php?eid=11436588798">
    Google I/O</a>
```

Google I/O

Figure 3-17. The result of our <fb:eventlink/> example

<fb:grouplink/>

```
<fb:grouplink gid="..."/>
```

Renders a link to a specified group on Facebook.

FBML-Specific Attributes

Required

`gid=[string] default: none`
: The group ID for the group to link to.

Optional

None.

Example FBML

Here is example FBML code for `<fb:grouplink/>`. This will link to the Utah Facebook Developers Garage group:

```
<fb:grouplink gid="3340942167"/>
```

Rendered HTML for Single Instance of Tag

The underlying HTML for the example looks like this (Figure 3-18 shows the result):

```
<a href="http://www.facebook.com/group.php?gid=3340942167">
    Utah Facebook Developers Garage</a>
```

Utah Facebook Developers Garage

Figure 3-18. The result of our <fb:grouplink/> example

<fb:networklink/>

```
<fb:networklink nid="..."/>
```

Renders a link to the specified Facebook network.

FBML-Specific Attributes

Required

`nid=[string] default: none`
: The network ID of the Facebook network to link to.

Optional

None.

Example FBML

Here is example FBML code for `<fb:networklink/>`. This will produce a link to the "Facebook" network:

```
<fb:networklink nid="50431648"/>
```

Rendered HTML for Single Instance of Tag

The underlying HTML for the example looks like this (Figure 3-19 shows the result):

```
<a href="http://www.facebook.com/networks/50431648/Facebook/">
    Facebook</a>
```

Facebook

Figure 3-19. The result of our <fb:networklink/> example

<fb:application-name/>

`<fb:application-name/>`

Renders the name of the current application. This is a good way to ensure that your application name will always be correct, even if you change the name of your app in the future.

FBML-Specific Attributes

Required

None.

Optional

None.

Example FBML

Here is the FBML code for `<fb:application-name/>` (yes, it's simple):

```
<fb:application-name/>
```

Rendered HTML for Single Instance of Tag

The rendered HTML would look like this for the FBML Essentials application on Facebook:

```
FBML Essentials
```

Additional Information

- This tag may be used for feed items.

HTML Display and Navigation

The following sections cover general HTML display tags and page navigation tags.

General HTML Display Tags

<fb:title/>

```
<fb:title>...</fb:title>
```

When placed anywhere in a canvas page, this sets the `<title/>` tag in HTML for a specific canvas page.

FBML-Specific Attributes

Required

None.

Optional

None.

Example FBML

Here is the FBML code for `<fb:title/>` used in the FBML Essentials app:

```
<fb:title>O'Reilly FBML Essentials - Examples, Tips, Tricks, and
    Trivia About Facebook!</fb:title>
```

Rendered HTML for Single Instance of Tag

The example produces a title tag that looks like the following in `<header/>` in the canvas page's HTML (Figure 3-20 shows the result):

```
<title>O'Reilly FBML Essentials - Examples, Tips, Tricks, and
    Trivia About Facebook!</title>
```

Facebook | FBML Essentials | O'Reilly FBML Essentials - Examples, Tips, Tricks, and Trivia About Facebook!

Figure 3-20. The title bar that results from our <fb:title/> example

Additional Information

- This tag works only on canvas pages. It will not work on a user's profile page.

<fb:iframe/>

```
<fb:iframe src="..."/>
```

An excellent tool when you need to render complex JavaScript, Flash, or unsupported FBML. This tag links to an external web address and renders the content from that URL inside an HTML `<iframe/>` tag on the canvas page. From the external URL, any HTML, JavaScript, or Flash may be used, but keep in mind that content will not be parsed by Facebook, and therefore FBML will not be supported for anything output by the `<fb:iframe/>` tags. `<fb:iframe/>` is not supported on user profile pages.

FBML-Specific Attributes

Required

`src=[`*`string`*`] default: none`
: External URL (non-Facebook, e.g., your own servers) to render in the iframe. All Facebook variables mentioned in the "Forms in FBML" section in Chapter 2 are appended to this URL, including `fb_sig_profile`, `fb_sig_user`, `fb_sig_session_key`, `fb_sig_time`, and `fb_sig`, in addition to an `fb_sig_in_iframe` parameter to let the app know it is being called from an iframe.

Optional

`smartsize=[true|false] default: false`
: If `true`, automatically fits the iframe to the remaining space on the page and disables the scrollbars.

`frameborder=[1|0] default: 1`
: If `1`, shows the iframe border. If 0, hides it.

`scrolling=[yes|no|auto] default: yes`
: If `yes`, displays scrollbars. If `no`, doesn't display scrollbars. If `auto`, scrollbars are displayed only if the enclosed content exceeds the size of the iframe.

`style=[`*`string`*`] default: none`
: Specifies the style for the iframe.

`width=[`*`int`*`] default: none`
: Specifies the width of the iframe.

`height=[int] default: none`
: Specifies the height of the iframe.

`resizable=[true|false] default: false`
: If `true`, allows the containing site to control the outer iframe's size via JavaScript. Cannot be used when `smartsize` is `true`. You must also specify a `name` attribute when using the `resizable` attribute. Please see Chapter 4 for more functional examples that show how to do this.

`name=[string] default: none`
: Name for the iframe. For use when `resizable="true"`, and enables access via JavaScript from the containing site.

Example FBML

Here is example FBML code for `<fb:iframe/>`:

```
<fb:iframe src="http://fbmlessentials.staynalive.com/?action=
    iframe&src=true& notabs=1" frameborder="1" width="100"
    height="100" style="margin:10px" scrolling="auto"/>
```

Rendered HTML for Single Instance of Tag

The generated `<fb:iframe/>` tag for the example looks like this (Figure 3-21 shows the result):

```
<iframe
  src="http://fbmlessentials.staynalive.com/?action=iframe&amp;
        src=true&amp;notabs=1&amp;
    fb_sig_in_iframe=1&amp;fb_sig_time=1205793218.0177&amp;
        fb_sig_added=0&amp;fb_sig_user=683545112&amp;
    fb_sig_profile_update_time=1205648428&amp;fb_sig_session_key=
        54aeab3103ef387539a31aa1-683545112&amp;
    fb_sig_expires=0&amp;fb_sig_api_key=
        ba19d367e2d8c4ea5813d54f2cbba136&amp;
    fb_sig=61cce193ae9cdc2cb2e2858481ea8cc9"
    frameborder="1"
    width="500"
    height="100"
    style="margin: 10px;"
    scrolling="auto">
</iframe>
```

Additional Information

- `<fb:iframe/>` works only on canvas pages. It will not work on a user's profile page.
- Be sure to use your own external, non-Facebook URL—i.e., the callback URL you specified in your application settings—for the `src`. If you don't, the iframe will wrap the Facebook look and feel.
- FBML is not supported within the iframe.

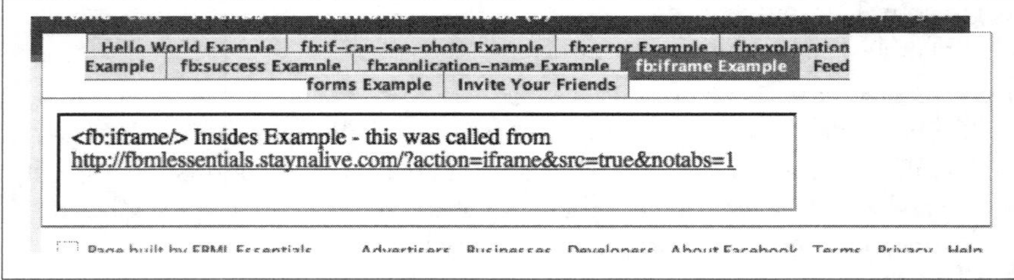

Figure 3-21. The result of our <fb:iframe/> example

Page Navigation Tags

<fb:dashboard/>

```
<fb:dashboard>...[<fb:action/>][<fb:create-button/>][<fb:help/>]
    </fb:dashboard>
```

Renders a standard Facebook dashboard header that works on canvas pages. This header provides links at the top of the page, and if the application has an icon, it will include that icon next to your application's name as part of the header.

FBML-Specific Attributes

Required

None.

Optional

None.

Example FBML

Here is example FBML code for <fb:dashboard/>, taken from the FBML Essentials app:

```
<fb:dashboard>
  <fb:action href="http://apps.facebook.com/fbmlessentials"
      title="Home">Home</fb:action>
  <fb:action href="http://apps.facebook.com/facebookquiz"
      title="How much do you know about Facebook?"> How much do you
      know about Facebook? </fb:action>
  <fb:help href="http://apps.facebook.com/fbmlessentials/?action=help"
      title="Get Help with this app">Help</fb:help>
  <fb:create-button href="http://apps.facebook.com/fbmlessentials/
      invite.php">Invite another Friend</fb:create-button>
</fb:dashboard>
```

Rendered HTML for Single Instance of Tag

The underlying HTML for the example looks like this (see Figure 3-22):

```
<div class="dashboard_header">
  <div class="dh_links clearfix">
    <div class="dh_actions">
      <a href="http://apps.facebook.com/fbmlessentials">Home</a>
      <span class="pipe">|</span>
      <a href="http://apps.facebook.com/facebookquiz">
      How much do you know about Facebook?</a>
    </div>
    <div class="dh_help">
      <a href="http://apps.facebook.com/fbmlessentials/?action=help">
          Help</a>
    </div>
  </div>
  <div class="dh_titlebar clearfix">
    <h2 style="background-image: url('http://static.ak.facebook.com/
        images/icons/hidden.gif?57:27651')">
    FBML Essentials
    </h2>
  </div>
  <div class="dh_new_media_shell">
    <a href="http://apps.facebook.com/fbmlessentials/invite.php"
        class="dh_new_media">
      <div class="tr">
        <div class="bl">
          <div class="br">
            <span>Invite another Friend</span>
          </div>
        </div>
      </div>
    </a>
  </div>
</div>
```

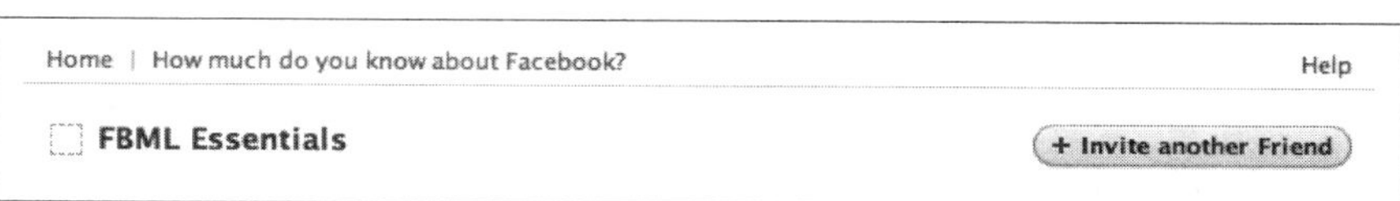

Figure 3-22. The result of our <fb:dashboard/> example

Additional Information

- `<fb:dashboard/>` works only on canvas pages.
- This tag supports the `<fb:action/>`, `<fb:create-button/>`, and `<fb:help/>` tags. See the descriptions of those tags later in this chapter for more information.
- `<fb:if-user-has-added/>` does not work within an `<fb:dashboard/>` tag, but it can be used to contain the tag.

<fb:action/>

```
[<fb:dashboard>|<fb:subtitle>]<fb:action href="...">...</fb:action>
    [</fb:dashboard>|</fb:subtitle>]
```

Renders a link on the right of an `<fb:subtitle/>` tag or on the left of an `<fb:dashboard/>` tag. See the `<fb:subtitle/>` and `<fb:dashboard/>` tags earlier in this chapter for context. `<fb:action/>` works the same—but looks different—in both instances.

FBML-Specific Attributes

Required

`href=[`*`string`*`] default: none`
: The URL for the link. This URL must be a Facebook canvas page (e.g., *apps.facebook.com...*).

Optional

`title=[`*`string`*`] default: none`
: Tool tip title for a link.

`onclick=[`*`string`*`] default: none`
: FBJS function to call when a link is clicked.

Example FBML

Here is example FBML code for `<fb:action/>`; please refer to the `<fb:subtitle/>` tag for context (Figure 3-23 shows the result):

```
<fb:action href="http://apps.facebook.com/fbmlessentials"
    title="Home">Home</fb:action>
```

Home | Purchase the Book!

Figure 3-23. The <fb:action/> tag in an <fb:subtitle/> tag rendered on a user's profile

Here is another example; please refer to the `<fb:dashboard/>` tag for context (Figure 3-24 shows the result):

```
<fb:action href="http://apps.facebook.com/facebookquiz"
    title="How much do you know about Facebook?">
    How much do you know about Facebook?
</fb:action>
```

Home | How much do you know about Facebook?

Figure 3-24. The <fb:action/> tag in an <fb:dashboard/> tag rendered on the canvas page

Additional Information

- This tag appears to the right of an `<fb:subtitle/>` tag and to the left of an `<fb:dashboard/>` tag.
- When used in an `<fb:subtitle/>` tag, this tag works only on the user's profile. When used in an `<fb:dashboard/>` tag, it works only on a canvas page.

<fb:create-button/>

```
<fb:dashboard>...<fb:create-button href="...">...</fb:create-button>
    </fb:dashboard>
```

Renders a special "Create" button that appears to the right of the title in an `<fb:dashboard/>` tag. The button is rounded, has a + symbol on the left side, and can contain any text you place between the tags.

FBML-Specific Attributes

Required

`href=[`*`string`*`] default: none`
: The canvas page within Facebook to link to. It must be of the *http://apps.facebook.com...* domain.

Optional

`title=[`*`string`*`] default: none`
: Text that appears when you hover over the "Create" button.

`onclick=[`*`string`*`] default: none`
: When clicked, calls the specified FBJS function.

Example FBML

Here is example FBML code for `<fb:create-button/>`, which generates a "Create" button in the upper-right corner of the canvas page:

```
<fb:dashboard>
  <fb:create-button href="http://apps.facebook.com/fbmlessentials/
      invite.php">Invite another Friend</fb:create-button>
</fb:dashboard>
```

Rendered HTML for Single Instance of Tag

The underlying HTML for the example looks like this (Figure 3-25 shows the result):

```
<div class="dh_new_media_shell">
    <a href="http://apps.facebook.com/fbmlessentials/invite.php"
        class="dh_new_media">
```

```
        <div class="tr">
          <div class="bl">
            <div class="br">
              <span>Invite another Friend</span>
            </div>
          </div>
        </div>
      </a>
    </div>
```

Figure 3-25. The result of our <fb:create-button/> example

Additional Information

- This tag works only on the canvas page.
- It must link to a canvas page.
- Only one "Create" button per canvas page is allowed.
- There is no way to remove the + symbol from the button.

<fb:help/>

`<fb:help href="...">...</fb:help>`

Renders a "Help" link with specified text that links to a specified help location. This tag works within an `<fb:dashboard/>` tag (described earlier in this chapter).

FBML-Specific Attributes

Required

`href=[`*`string`*`] default: none`
    Location to send the user to when they click on the "Help" link.

Optional

`title=[`*`string`*`] default: none`
    Tool tip text to show upon mouseover of the link.

Example FBML

Here is example FBML code for `<fb:help/>`:

```
<fb:dashboard>
  <fb:help href="http://apps.facebook.com/fbmlessentials/?action=help"
      title="Get Help with this app"/>
</fb:dashboard>
```

Rendered HTML for Single Instance of Tag

The underlying HTML for the example looks like this (Figure 3-26 shows the result):

```
<div class="dh_help">
  <a href="http://apps.facebook.com/fbmlessentials/?action=help">
  Help</a></div>
```

Help

Figure 3-26. Our <fb:help/> example produces a link in the dashboard

Additional Information

- This tag works only in an `<fb:dashboard/>` tag.

<fb:header/>

`<fb:header>...</fb:header>`

Renders a header title in place of the tag, and optionally places the application's icon next to the header text.

FBML-Specific Attributes

Required

None.

Optional

`icon=[true|false] default: true`
: If `true`, displays the application's icon next to the header text.

`decoration=[add_border|no_padding|shorten] default: none`
: If `add_border`, it adds a 1-pixel, solid `#ccc`-colored border below the header. If `no_padding`, it removes the 20 pixels of padding around the header. If `shorten`, it removes the 20 pixels of padding below the header.

Example FBML

The following example FBML code for `<fb:header/>` produces a standard Facebook header (using the text, *"Hello Friends" Example*), along with the application icon and all the styling that goes with it:

```
<fb:header>"Hello Friends" Example</fb:header>
```

Rendered HTML for Single Instance of Tag

The underlying HTML for the example looks like this (Figure 3-27 shows the result):

```
<div class="title_header">
  <h2 class="" style="background-image: url(http://
       static.ak.facebook.com/images/icons/hidden.gif?57:27651)">
    &quot;Hello Friends&quot; Example
  </h2>
</div>
```

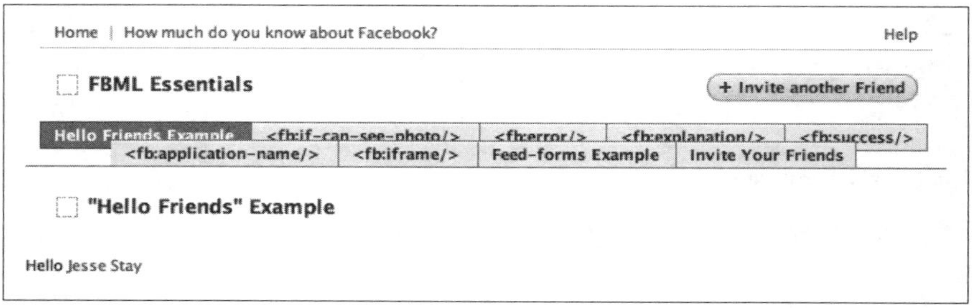

Figure 3-27. The result of our <fb:header/> example

<fb:mediaheader/>

```
<fb:mediaheader uid="...">[<fb:owner-action>...</fb:owner-action>]
    [<fb:header-title>...</fb:header-title>]</fb:mediaheader>
```

Renders a special header that includes a picture of the specified user, along with a "Profile" link, a "Send Message" link, or a "Poke" link. Additionally, customized links can be set up (using the `<fb:owner-action/>` tag) that display only if the current user is the same as the user specified. In such a case, the "Profile," "Send Message," and "Poke" links are all replaced with the specified `<fb:owner-action/>` link.

FBML-Specific Attributes

Required

`uid=[`*`string`*`] default: none`
    The ID of the Facebook user to render the media header for.

Optional

None.

Example FBML

Here is example FBML code for `<fb:mediaheader/>`; it renders differently depending on whether you are the user with the specified ID (as shown in Figure 3-28) or not (as shown in Figure 3-29):

```
<fb:mediaheader uid="4">
  <fb:owner-action href="http://apps.facebook.com/fbmlessentials/">
      View Your Messages.</fb:owner-action>
  <fb:header-title>&lt;fb:mediaheader/&gt; Example</fb:header-title>
</fb:mediaheader>
```

Figure 3-28. The result of the <fb:mediaheader/> example if your user ID is 4

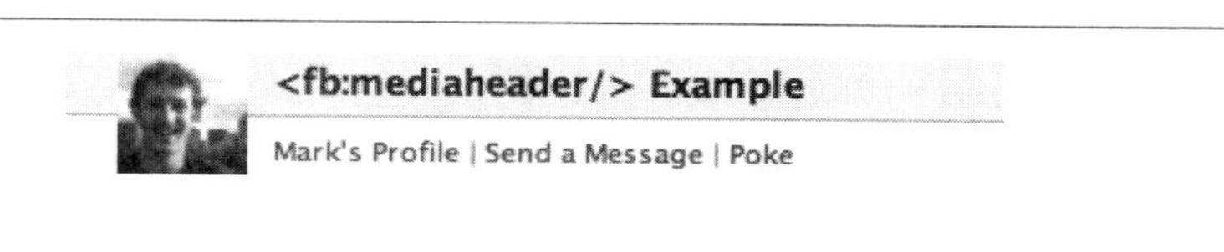

Figure 3-29. The result of the <fb:mediaheader/> example if you are anyone else

Additional Information

- This tag must have room to span across the entire canvas.
- This tag does not work in profile boxes.

<fb:header-title/>

`<fb:header-title>...</fb:header-title>`

The text to display as the title for an `<fb:mediaheader/>` tag. See `<fb:mediaheader/>` (described previously) for an example. Simply add the text you want to display in between the tags.

FBML-Specific Attributes

Required

None.

Optional

None.

Example FBML

Please see `<fb:mediaheader/>` earlier in this chapter for an example.

<fb:owner-action/>

```
<fb:owner-action href="...">...</fb:owner-action>
```

A link to display in place of the Profile, Send Message, and Poke links if the user viewing the app is the same as the specified user in an `<fb:mediaheader/>` tag.

FBML-Specific Attributes

Required

`href=[string] default: none`
: The URL to take the user to when they click on the link.

Optional

None.

Example FBML

Please see `<fb:mediaheader/>` earlier in this chapter for an example.

Additional Information

- This tag works only within an `<fb:mediaheader/>` tag.
- Multiple links can coexist in a single `<fb:mediaheader/>` tag.

<fb:tabs/>

```
<fb:tabs><fb:tab-item href="..." title="..."/>...</fb:tabs>
```

Renders a set of standard Facebook tabs for your app. The tabs appear wherever the tags are placed in the app. Please also see the `<fb:dashboard/>` tag (described earlier) for a different style of navigation.

FBML-Specific Attributes

Required

`href=[string] default: none`
: The URL to take the user to when they click on the link.

Optional

None.

Example FBML

The following example FBML code for `<fb:tabs/>` renders "Hello Friends Example" and "Invite Your Friends" tabs, with the first tab being selected:

```
<fb:tabs>
    <fb:tab-item href="http://apps.facebook.com/fbmlessentials/"
        title="Hello Friends Example" selected="true"/>
    <fb:tab-item href="http://apps.facebook.com/fbmlessentials/
        invite.php" title="Invite Your Friends" />
</fb:tabs>
```

Rendered HTML for Single Instance of Tag

The underlying HTML for the example looks like this (Figure 3-30 shows the result):

```
<div class="tabs clearfix"><center><div class="left_tabs">
   <ul class="toggle_tabs clearfix" id="toggle_tabs_unused">
   <li class="first "> <a href="http://apps.facebook.com/fbmlessentials/"
   class="selected"> Hello Friends Example </a></li><li class="last ">
   <a href="http://apps.facebook.com/fbmlessentials/invite.php">
   Invite Your Friends </a></li></ul></div></center></div>
```

Figure 3-30. The result of our <fb:tabs/> example

Additional Information

- Multiple `<fb:tabs/>` are allowed on a single canvas page.
- This tag must contain at least one `<fb:tab-item/>`.

<fb:tab-item/>

```
<fb:tab-item href="..." title="..."/>
```

Renders a single tab within an `<fb:tabs/>` tag.

FBML-Specific Attributes

Required

`href=[string] default: none`
: The location to take the user to when they click on the tab.

`title=[string] default: none`
: Text to display in the tab.

Optional

`selected=[true|false] default: false`
: If `true`, highlights the tab in blue (see the `<fb:tabs/>` example).

`align=[left|right] default: left`
: Specifies the alignment of the tab.

Try `align="right"` for "Help" and "Admin" tabs so that they stand out from the other left-aligned tabs.

Example FBML

Please see `<fb:tabs/>` earlier in this chapter for an example.

Additional Information

- Dynamic FBML (i.e., Mock AJAX and other added attributes) does not work with this tag.

<fb:share-button/>

```
<fb:share-button class="...">...</fb:share-button>
```

Takes a given target URL—optionally with some meta information so that it knows what to render—and displays a dialog box with a preview box of the target URL, inviting the user to share that content with friends. The "Share" button will automatically try to render the URL for you, or else you can provide metadata explicitly in the `share-button` call or in the site itself that tells Facebook how to display the preview.

FBML-Specific Attributes

Required

`class=[url|meta] default: none`
: The method to provide attributes to Facebook to aid in rendering the preview to be shared.

`href=[string] default: none`
: Required only when `class="url"` is used. This is the URL to render a preview for. The URL should contain meta elements (listed next) to provide the most intelligent preview possible.

Optional

If `meta` is selected for the `class` attribute, you must provide optional link and meta tags within the `<fb:share-button/>` tags.

Meta and Link Tags

The following are the accepted meta and link tags for different types of content.

Basic meta tags

These tags can be used with any content type. Be sure to include the `medium` meta tag to specify the type of content. You can create a preview of any page, not just audio and video sources, using these tags:

- `<meta name="title" content="`*`The title of the page`*`"/>`
- `<meta name="description" content="`*`The description of the content on the page`*`"/>`
- `<meta name="medium" content="[audio|image|video|news|blog|mult]"/>`
- `<link rel="image_src" content="`*`The URL of the image to be displayed`*`"/>`
- `<link rel="target_url" content="`*`The URL of the document being shared`*`"/>`

Required meta tags for an audio source

- `<meta name="title" content="`*`The title of the page`*`"/>`
- `<meta name="description" content="`*`The description of the audio`*`"/>`
- `<link rel="image_src" content="`*`The URL of the image (such as album art) for the audio`*`"/>`
- `<link rel="audio_src" content="`*`The URL of the audio file`*`"/>`
- `<meta name="audio_type" content="`*`Content-Type of the audio file`*`"/>`

Optional meta tags for an audio source

- `<meta name="audio_title" content="`*`The title of the audio (such as song name)`*`"/>`
- `<meta name="audio_artist" content="`*`The author of the audio (singer, rapper, speaker)`*`"/>`
- `<meta name="audio_album" content="`*`The album the audio belongs to`*`"/>`

Required meta tags for a video source

- `<meta name="title" content="`*`The title of the page`*`"/>`
- `<meta name="description" content="`*`The description of the page`*`"/>`

- `<link rel="image_src" content="`*`The URL of the image or screenshot of the video`*`"/>`
- `<link rel="video_src" content="`*`The URL of the video being previewed or shared`*`"/>`
- `<meta name="video_height" content="`*`The height of the video`*`"/>`
- `<meta name="video_width" content="`*`The width of the video`*`"/>`
- `<meta name="video_type" content="`*`Content-Type of the video file`*`"/>`

Example FBML

Here is an example of the `<fb:share-button/>` tag with meta information. For the following video:

```
<object width="425" height="355">
<param name="movie" value="http://www.youtube.com/v/I6IQ_FOCE6I&hl=en">
</param>
<param name="wmode" value="transparent">
</param>
<embed src="http://www.youtube.com/v/I6IQ_FOCE6I&hl=en"
    type="application/x-shockwave-flash" wmode="transparent"
    width="425" height="355">
</embed>
</object>
```

you would use this FBML code (note that I added my own screenshot in the `image_src` field):

```
<fb:share-button class="meta">
  <meta name="medium" content="video"/>
  <meta name="title" content="Here Comes Another Bubble v1.1"/>
  <meta name="description" content="Funny Video About the 'Social
      Media Bubble'"/>
  <link rel="image_src" href="http://staynalive.com/wp-content/
      themes/revvedup-158/images/Picture_1-20080318-164716.jpg"/>
  <link rel="video_src" href="http://www.youtube.com/v/
      I6IQ_FOCE6I&hl=en"/>
  <link rel="target_url" href="http://youtube.com/watch?v=
      I6IQ_FOCE6I"/>
  <meta name="video_height" content="355"/>
  <meta name="video_width" content="425"/>
  <meta name="video_type" content="application/x-shockwave-flash"/>
</fb:share-button>
```

Here is a second example of the `<fb:share-button/>` tag, this time with just a URL:

```
<fb:share-button class="url" href="http://youtube.com/watch?v=
    I6IQ_FOCE6I"/>
```

Rendered HTML for Single Instance of Tag

Both examples will render as shown in Figure 3-31. (Note that the example with just a URL would autopopulate its own screenshot from the first image on the page or from existing meta tags.) The "Share" button that generates this image when clicked is shown in Figure 3-32.

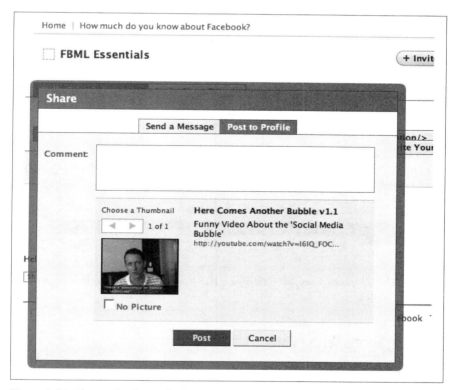

Figure 3-31. The result of our <fb:share-button/> examples

Figure 3-32. The "Share" button

<fb:page-admin-edit-header/>

```
<fb:page-admin-edit-header/>
```

Adds a canvas-only header that makes it easy for page admins to manage the page an app belongs to. This tag works only on canvas pages of apps that have been added to a Facebook Page of which the user is an admin.

FBML-Specific Attributes

Required

None.

Optional

None.

Example FBML

This tag is very simple. It just looks like this:

```
<fb:page-admin-edit-header/>
```

If you are an admin of a Facebook Page that this app belongs to, you'll see something like Figure 3-33 (taken from *http://wiki.developers.facebook.com/index.php/Fb:page-admin-edit-header*).

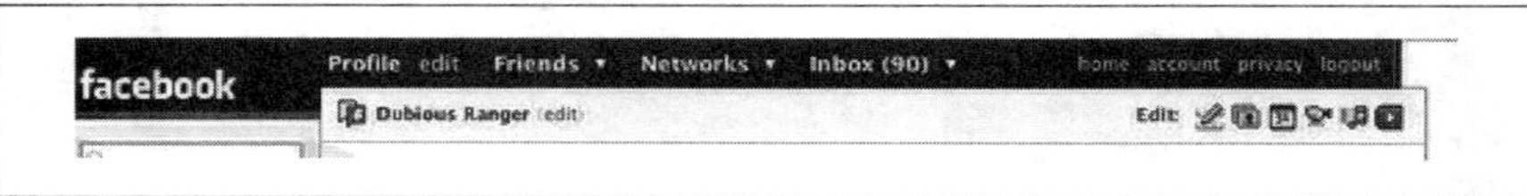

Figure 3-33. The result from our <fb:page-admin-edit-header/> example if you are an admin

Creating Forms With FBML

<fb:editor/>

```
<fb:editor action="...">...</fb:editor>
```

Renders a special Facebook-formatted form with two columns. This is a great way to render a form that matches the standard Facebook look and feel. For more complex operations for a form, I strongly suggest you just use a standard HTML `<form/>` tag. See also the following tags elsewhere in this chapter:

- `<fb:editor-button/>`
- `<fb:editor-buttonset/>`
- `<fb:editor-cancel/>`
- `<fb:editor-custom/>`
- `<fb:editor-date/>`
- `<fb:editor-divider/>`
- `<fb:editor-month/>`

- `<fb:editor-text/>`
- `<fb:editor-textarea/>`
- `<fb:editor-time/>`

FBML-Specific Attributes

Required

`action=[*string*] default: none`
: The location to send the form to. Note that all `<fb:editor/>` forms are sent via the POST form method, so be sure you authenticate properly with that in mind!

Optional

`width=[*int*] default: none`
: The width of the form as a whole. (The form renders a table—this is the table's width.)

`labelwidth=[*int*] default: none`
: The width of the labels in the form (the left column). The right column will adjust based on the width value of `<fb:editor/>`.

Example FBML

Here is example FBML code for a form using `<fb:editor/>`:

```
<fb:editor action="http://apps.facebook.com/fbmlessentials">
  <fb:editor-custom>
    <input type="hidden" name="action" value="editor" />
    <input type="hidden" name="submit" value="true" />
  </fb:editor-custom>
  <fb:editor-text label="Your Name" name="name" value=""/>
  <fb:editor-textarea label="Your Address" name="address" value=""/>
  <fb:editor-date label="Your Birthday" name="birthday"/>
  <fb:editor-month label="Current Month" name="month"/>
  <fb:editor-time label="Current Time" name="time"/>
  <fb:editor-divider/>
  <fb:editor-buttonset>
    <fb:editor-button name="submit" value="Submit Name"/>
    <fb:editor-cancel name="cancel" value="Cancel"/>
  </fb:editor-buttonset>
</fb:editor>
```

Rendered HTML for Single Instance of Tag

The underlying HTML looks like the following (Figure 3-34 shows the result). This is important because if you need Mock AJAX or a GET request, you have to render your own form:

```
<form action="http://apps.facebook.com/fbmlessentials" method="post">
  <table class="editorkit" border="0" cellspacing="0" style="width:425px">
  <tr class="width_setter">
    <th style="width:75px"></th>
    <td></td>
  </tr>
  <tr>
    <th class="detached_label"><label></label></th>
    <td class="editorkit_row">
      <input type="hidden" name="action" value="editor" />
      <input type="hidden" name="submit" value="true" />
    </td>
    <td class="right_padding"></td>
  </tr>
  <tr>
    <th><label>Your Name:</label></th>
    <td class="editorkit_row"><input type="text" name="name"/></td>
    <td class="right_padding"></td>
  </tr>
  <tr>
    <th class="detached_label">
      <label>Your Address:</label>
    </th>
    <td class="editorkit_row"><textarea name="address"></textarea></td>
    <td class="right_padding"></td>
  </tr>
  <tr>
    <th><label>Your Birthday:</label></th>
    <td class="editorkit_row">
      <select name="birthday_month" id="birthday_month"
      onchange="editor_date_month_change(this, 'birthday_day','');" >
        <option value="1">Jan</option><option value="2">Feb</option>
        <option value="3">Mar</option><option value="4">Apr</option>
        <option value="5">May</option><option value="6">Jun</option>
        <option value="7">Jul</option><option value="8">Aug</option>
        <option value="9">Sep</option><option value="10">Oct</option>
        <option value="11">Nov</option>
        <option value="12" selected>Dec</option>
      </select>
      <select name="birthday_day" id="birthday_day">
      <option value="1">1</option><option value="2">2</option>
      <option value="3">3</option><option value="4">4</option>
      <option value="5">5</option><option value="6">6</option>
      <option value="7">7</option><option value="8">8</option>
      <option value="9">9</option><option value="10">10</option>
      <option value="11">11</option><option value="12">12</option>
      <option value="13">13</option><option value="14">14</option>
          <option value="15">15</option>
      <option value="16">16</option><option value="17">17</option>
          <option value="18">18</option>
      <option value="19">19</option><option value="20">20</option>
          <option value="21">21</option>
      <option value="22">22</option><option value="23">23</option>
          <option value="24">24</option>
```

```
      <option value="25">25</option><option value="26">26</option>
          <option value="27">27</option>
      <option value="28">28</option><option value="29">29</option>
          <option value="30">30</option>
      <option value="31" selected>31</option>
      </select>
    </td>
    <td class="right_padding"></td>
  </tr>
  <tr>
    <th><label>Current Month:</label></th>
    <td class="editorkit_row">
      <select name="month" id="month"  >
        <option value="-1">Month:</option><option value="1">Jan</option>
            <option value="2">Feb</option>
        <option value="3">Mar</option><option value="4">Apr</option>
            <option value="5">May</option>
        <option value="6">Jun</option><option value="7">Jul</option>
            <option value="8">Aug</option>
        <option value="9">Sep</option><option value="10">Oct</option>
            <option value="11">Nov</option>
        <option value="12">Dec</option>
      </select>
    </td>
    <td class="right_padding"></td>
  </tr>
  <tr>
    <th><label>Current Time:</label></th>
    <td class="editorkit_row">
      <select name="time_hour" id="time_hour">
        <option value="1">1</option><option value="2">2</option>
            <option value="3">3</option>
        <option value="4" selected>4</option><option value="5">5</option>
            <option value="6">6</option>
        <option value="7">7</option><option value="8">8</option>
            <option value="9">9</option>
        <option value="10">10</option><option value="11">11</option>
            <option value="12">12</option>
      </select><span>:</span>
      <select name="time_min" id="time_min">
        <option value="00" selected>00</option><option value="05">05</option>
        <option value="10">10</option><option value="15">15</option>
            <option value="20">20</option>
        <option value="25">25</option><option value="30">30</option>
            <option value="35">35</option>
        <option value="40">40</option><option value="45">45</option>
            <option value="50">50</option>
        <option value="55">55</option></select><select name="time_ampm"
            id="time_ampm">
        <option value="am">am</option><option value="pm" selected>pm</option>
      </select>
    </td>
    <td class="right_padding"></td>
  </tr>
```

```
    <tr><th></th><td colspan="2"><div class="divider"></div></td></tr>
    <tr><th></th><td class="editorkit_buttonset">
      <input type="submit" class="editorkit_button action" value="Submit Name"
          name="submit" />
      <span class="cancel_link"><span>or</span><a href="#">Cancel</a></span>
    </td><td class="right_padding"></td></tr>
    </table>
  </form>
```

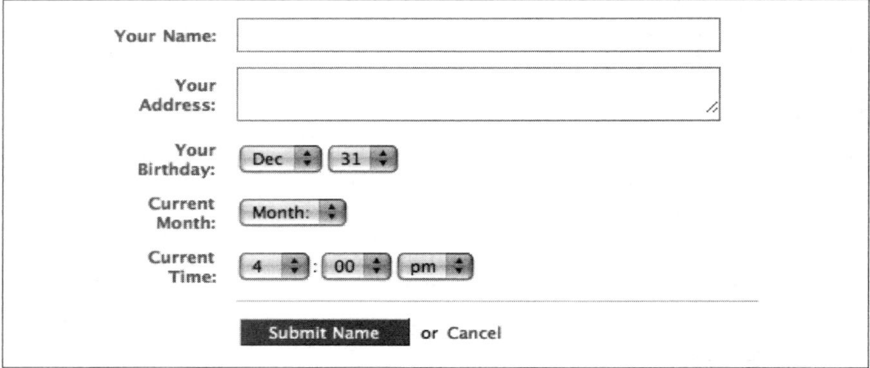

Figure 3-34. The result of our <fb:editor/> form example

Additional Information

- `<fb:editor/>` forms do *not* work with Mock AJAX. Use a normal form (see the HTML example just shown) to make it work.
- `<fb:editor/>` forms get sent via POST methods.

<fb:editor-buttonset/>

`<fb:editor-buttonset>...</fb:editor-buttonset>`

Produces a set of buttons for an `<fb:editor/>` form. To be used with either an `<fb:button/>` or `<fb:cancel/>` tag.

FBML-Specific Attributes

Required

None.

Optional

None.

Example FBML

Please see the `<fb:editor/>` tag earlier in this chapter for an example.

Additional Information

- This tag must contain at least one `<fb:editor-button/>` as a child.

<fb:editor-button/>

```
<fb:editor-button value="..."/>
```

Produces a standard input button within an `<fb:editor-buttonset/>` or by itself on an `<fb:editor/>` form. When used by itself, it does not get styled as a regular editor button.

FBML-Specific Attributes

Required

`value=[`*string*`] default:none`
: Form field value for the submit button. Also the text that renders on the submit button.

Optional

`name=[`*string*`] default:none`
: The name of the form field (used for DOM access in FBJS and for your server-side scripts).

Example FBML

Please see the `<fb:editor/>` tag earlier in this chapter for an example.

<fb:editor-cancel/>

```
<fb:editor-cancel value="..."/>
```

Renders a cancel button for an `<fb:editor/>` form, within an `<fb:editor-buttonset/>` if with a group of buttons, or by itself if not.

FBML-Specific Attributes

Required

`value=[`*string*`] default: none`
: Form value for the cancel button. Also, the text to display in the button.

Optional

`href=[#|string] default: #`
: The URL to redirect the user to if they click the cancel button.

Example FBML

Please see the `<fb:editor/>` tag earlier in this chapter for an example.

<fb:editor-custom/>

`<fb:editor-custom>...</fb:editor-custom>`

Allows for custom tags within `<fb:editor/>`. Any valid FBML tag is allowed. It works great for placing hidden input form elements and checkboxes, or just plain text, as a row in the `<fb:editor/>` box.

FBML-Specific Attributes

Required

None.

Optional

`label=[string] default: none`
: Label that goes in the lefthand column for the `<fb:editor-custom/>` tag. All content between the tags will go in the righthand column.

`id=[string] default: none`
: The ID for the element to be accessed by FBJS.

Example FBML

Please see the `<fb:editor/>` tag earlier in this chapter for an example.

<fb:editor-date/>

`<fb:editor-date label="..."/>`

Renders a set of `<select/>` tags that provide a day drop-down menu and a month drop-down menu, which can be read as dates by the POSTed script.

FBML-Specific Attributes

Required

`label=[string] default: none`
: The string of text to display in the left column of the `<fb:editor/>` form.

Optional

`value=[int] default: Dec. 31 converted to UNIX timestamp`
: The UNIX timestamp to set the date drop-downs to when the page loads.

Example FBML

Please see the `<fb:editor/>` tag earlier in this chapter for an example.

Additional Information

- When the form is posted, two attributes are submitted:

  `date_month`
  : The month value, i.e., a number between 1 and 12.

  `date_day`
  : The day value, i.e., a number between 1 and 31.
- More than one `<fb:editor-date/>` submits only the last set in the form. Use `<fb:editor-custom/>` to use more than one date selector. (See the example HTML for the `<fb:editor/>` tag earlier in this chapter.)
- External validation should be performed, as nothing checks for illegal dates (such as February 30).
- When you are posting to the same page, the previous selection does not stay selected.

<fb:editor-divider/>

```
<fb:editor-divider/>
```

Creates a divider line between elements of an `<fb:editor/>` form. Translates to a `<div/>` tag with a class of `divider`.

FBML-Specific Attributes

Required

None.

Optional

None.

Example FBML

Please see the `<fb:editor/>` tag earlier in this chapter for an example.

<fb:editor-month/>

`<fb:editor-month/>`

Produces a drop-down menu of January through December for the month within `<fb:editor/>` tags.

FBML-Specific Attributes

Optional

`name=[month|`*`string`*`] default: month`
: The name to provide to the form element in the form; gets passed on in the POST variables.

`value=[Month:|`*`int`*`] default: Month:`
: The value at which to set the month, from 1–12 (1 = January, 12 = December). In the POST variables, if `Month:` is selected, -1 gets passed back to the form.

Example FBML

Please see the `<fb:editor/>` tag earlier in this chapter for an example.

<fb:editor-text/>

`<fb:editor-text/>`

Produces a standard form text input within `<fb:editor/>` tags.

FBML-Specific Attributes

Required

None.

Optional

`label=[`*`string`*`] default: none`
: The text to display in the left column as a label for the row.

`name=[string] default: none`
: The name to pass back to the POST variables.

`value=[string] default: none`
: The value to assign to the name in the POST variables; appears in the text box on form load.

`maxlength=[string] default: none`
: The max length of the text input box in the form.

Example FBML

Please see the `<fb:editor/>` tag earlier in this chapter for an example.

<fb:editor-textarea/>

`<fb:editor-textarea>...</fb:editor-textarea>`

Renders a standard form `<textarea/>` tag in an `<fb:editor/>` form.

FBML-Specific Attributes

Required

None.

Optional

`label=[string] default: none`
: The label text for the left column of the `<fb:editor/>` form.

`name=[string] default: none`
: The name of the `<textarea/>` form input to submit back to the POST variables.

`rows=[string] default: none`
: Same as a real `<textarea/>` tag; specifies the number of rows to display (size).

Example FBML

Please see the `<fb:editor/>` tag earlier in this chapter for an example.

Additional Information

To include a value in the `<textarea/>` tag, place it between the `<fb:editor-textarea/>` tags.

<fb:editor-time/>

`<fb:editor-time/>`

Produces three drop-down menus for the hour, minute, and a.m./p.m. of the day within an `<fb:editor/>` form.

FBML-Specific Attributes

Required

None.

Optional

`label=[string] default: none`
: The label text to include on the left column of the `<fb:editor/>` form.

`name=[time|string] default: time`
: The name within the form to send as a POST variable when the form is submitted and to use within FBJS.

`value=[string] default: none`
: The value to set in epoch seconds of what the drop-downs will be set to when the page loads.

Example FBML

Please see the `<fb:editor/>` tag earlier in this chapter for an example.

Additional Information

- The three drop-downs send three POST variables:

  `name_hour`
  : The hour of the day

  `name_min`
  : The minute of the hour

  `name_ampm`
  : The section of the day

- The selector is rounded to the nearest 15 minutes.
- The drop-downs show only the time, not the date.

<fb:captcha/>

```
<fb:captcha/>
```

An element within `<form/>` tags, this tag places a "reCAPTCHA" image within the form that contains two pieces of text that must be entered into a text input by the user. The form gets redirected back to the URL in the `action` parameter for the form with the additional parameter `fb_sig_captcha_grade` appended, which lets your app know whether the CAPTCHA entry was successful.

As a developer, you can feel proud to include reCAPTCHAs in your apps, not only because they help reduce spam on Facebook, but because every entry is a contribution back to the Archive.org project (*http://www.archive.org*). One of the words in the Facebook reCAPTCHA is always a word from a document scanned by Archive.org, and so your users are transcribing that text one word at a time. See *http://recaptcha.net* for more information on how the reCAPTCHA that Facebook uses works.

FBML-Specific Attributes

Required

None.

Optional

`showalways=[true|false] default: none`
: If `true`, the CAPTCHA will appear every single time the user visits the form, regardless of whether the user previously passed the CAPTCHA test. If `false`, the CAPTCHA will appear only until the user passes the test once.

Example FBML

Here is example FBML code for `<fb:captcha/>`:

```
<form action="http://fbmlessentials.staynalive.com" method="post">
  <fb:captcha showalways="true"/>
  <input type="submit" value="Submit Query" />
</form>
```

Rendered HTML for Single Instance of Tag

The example produces a CAPTCHA box that looks like the one in Figure 3-35.

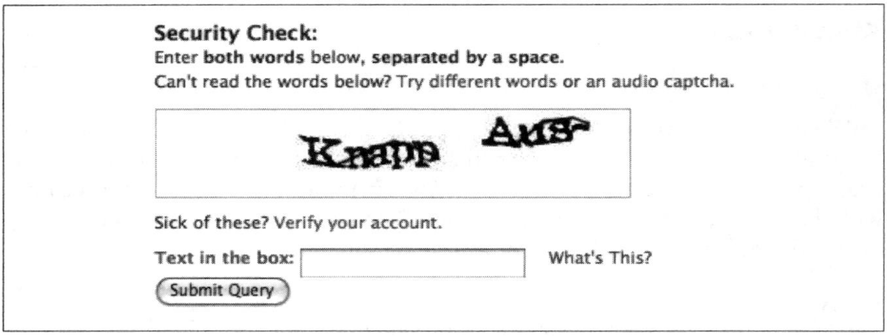

Figure 3-35. The result of our <fb:captcha/> example

Additional Information

- `fb_sig_captcha_grade` will be appended to the URL you pass to the `action` parameter within your form. If it returns `1`, the user passed the CAPTCHA test. If it returns `0`, the user did not pass. It is your application's responsibility to handle this parameter appropriately.

<fb:submit/>

`<fb:submit>...</fb:submit>`

For any image or text between the tags, this tag turns them into a form submit button. When a `form_id` is specified, it submits the identified form. Otherwise, if within an existing form, it will submit the form it is part of.

FBML-Specific Attributes

Required

None.

Optional

`form_id=[`*`string`*`] default: none`
: The ID of a form to submit. With this, the tag does not need to be within normal `<form/>` elements.

Example FBML

Here is example FBML code for `<fb:submit/>` (taken from the Developer Wiki):

```
<fb:submit><img src="http://images.jupiterimages.com/common/
    detail/50/17/22851750.jpg"></fb:submit>
```

<fb:typeahead-input/>

```
<fb:fbml version="1.1"><fb:typeahead-input name="...">...
    <fb:typeahead-option value="...">...</fb:typeahead-option>
    </fb:typeahead-input></fb:fbml>
```

Renders a type-ahead text input box that autodetects what the user is typing and tries to match a drop-down menu of options with what the user is typing. A good example of this can be seen in the search box in the upper-left corner of the Facebook site. At the time of this writing, this tag is currently in beta and therefore requires the `<fb:fbml version="1.1"/>` tags wrapped around it.

FBML-Specific Attributes

Required

`name=[`*`string`*`] default: none`
: The name to submit in the POST request with the form. The selected value in the input box will be passed with this name.

Optional

`autocomplete=[on|off] default: on`
: If `on`, allows the browser's autocomplete functions to override the autocomplete of the `<fb:typeahead-input/>` tag. It is recommended that you set this to `off` to override the browser functionality.

`value=[`*`string`*`] default: none`
: The default value to include in the input box when the page loads. Note that it doesn't translate to the text of the `<fb:typeahead-option/>` box it corresponds to.

Example FBML

Here is example FBML code for `<fb:typeahead-input/>`:

```
<form>
<fb:fbml version="1.1">
  <fb:typeahead-input name="name" autocomplete="off" value="mark">
    <fb:typeahead-option value="jesse">Jesse Stay</fb:typeahead-option>
    <fb:typeahead-option value="mark">Mark Zuckerberg</fb:typeahead-option>
    <fb:typeahead-option value="nick">Nick O'Neill</fb:typeahead-option>
  </fb:typeahead-input>
</fb:fbml>
</form>
```

Rendered HTML for Single Instance of Tag

The underlying HTML when rendered looks like this (Figure 3-36 shows the result):

```
<form>
<input type="hidden" name="name_val" id="name_val" />
<input name="name" autocomplete="off" value="mark" class="inputtext"
  onfocus="var source = new custom_source(
    [{&quot;i&quot;:&quot;jesse&quot;,&quot;t&quot;:&quot;
    Jesse Stay&quot;},{&quot;i&quot;:&quot;mark&quot;,&quot;
    t&quot;:&quot;Mark Zuckerberg&quot;},{&quot;i&quot;:&quot;
    nick&quot;,&quot;t&quot;:&quot;Nick O&#039;Neill&quot;}]);
    source.text_placeholder = null;
    var ta = new typeaheadpro(this, source, {onselect: function(
    row) { $(&quot;name_val&quot;).value = row.i; ; }});">
</form>
```

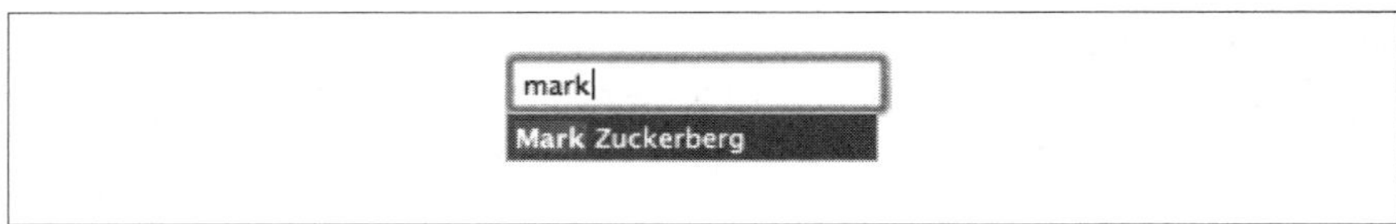

Figure 3-36. The result of our <fb:typeahead-input/> example

Additional Information

- Be sure to include this tag within a `<form/>` tag to have it submit with the form (or use FBJS).
- This tag must be included within an `<fbml version="1.1"/>` set of tags.
- This tag is currently under beta at the time of this writing.
- If none of the options are selected, the text entered in the input box gets sent back to the form.

<fb:typeahead-option/>

`<fb:typeahead-option>...</fb:typeahead-option>`

For use inside `<fb:typeahead-input/>` tags; specifies a single option to suggest to the user if their typing matches the containing text of the `<fb:typeahead-option/>` tag.

FBML-Specific Attributes

Required

None.

Optional

`value=[string] default: none`
: If specified, indicates the value to send with the POST in the `<fb:typeahead-input/>` tag.

Example FBML

Please see the `<fb:typeahead-input/>` tag earlier for an example.

<fb:friend-selector/>

`<fb:friend-selector/>`

A special `<fb:typeahead-input/>` box that renders a form input text box that autocompletes with a drop-down list of friends' names, which the user can select from. Only one friend can be chosen with this tag. To select multiple friends, use the `<fb:multi-friend-input/>` tag. This tag can be used inside and out of `<fb:request-form/>` tags.

FBML-Specific Attributes

Required

None.

Optional

`uid=[int] default: uid of current logged-in-user`
: The ID of the user to display a `<fb:friend-selector/>` input box for.

`name=[string] default: friend_selector_name`
: The name of the form element to submit with POST variables.

`idname=[string] default: friend_selector_id`
: The name of the hidden element within the form that displays the ID of the selected friend. If used within `<fb:request-form/>` tags, do not change it to anything other than `friend_selector_id`.

`include_me=[true|false] default: false`
: If `true`, includes the logged-in user in the list of friends to autocomplete.

`exclude_ids=[array] default: none`
: Comma-separated list of user IDs to exclude from the friend's list. This can be used within an `<fb:request-form/>` to exclude those friends who have already been invited.

`include_lists=[true|false] default: false`
: If `true`, includes friends lists in the drop-down list of suggested friends.

Example FBML

Here is example FBML code for `<fb:friend-selector/>`:

```
<form>
<fb:friend-selector name="my_friend" idname="my_friend_id"
    include_me="true" exclude_ids="4,1,2" include_lists="true"/>
</form>
```

Rendered HTML for Single Instance of Tag

The underlying HTML when rendered looks like this (Figure 3-37 shows the result):

```
<form>
  <input type="hidden" name="fb_sig_time" value="1206154647.8097" />
  <input type="hidden" name="fb_sig_added" value="0" />
  <input type="hidden" name="fb_sig_user" value="683545112" />
  <input type="hidden" name="fb_sig_profile_update_time"
      value="1205994295" />
  <input type="hidden" name="fb_sig_session_key"
      value="54aeab3103ef387539a31aa1-683545112" />
  <input type="hidden" name="fb_sig_expires" value="0" />
  <input type="hidden" name="fb_sig_api_key"
      value="ba19d367e2d8c4ea5813d54f2cbba136" />
  <input type="hidden" name="fb_sig"
      value="61014ec6e6d947973c28e2b823127bd2" />
  <input name="my_friend" idname="my_friend_id"
    value="Start typing a friend&#039;s name"
        class="inputtext typeahead_placeholder"
    maxlength="100" size="25" autocomplete="off" type="input"
    onfocus="var typeahead_source_instance1=
       new friend_source(
       &#039;683545112-1206123558-1&amp;u=683545112&amp;include_me=
       1&amp;lists=1&#039;);typeahead_source_instance1.set_exclude_ids(
       {&quot;4&quot;:true,&quot;1&quot;:true,&quot;2&quot;:true});
       new FBML.friendSelector(this, typeahead_source_instance1,{
       should_use_absolute:1});" />
</form>
```

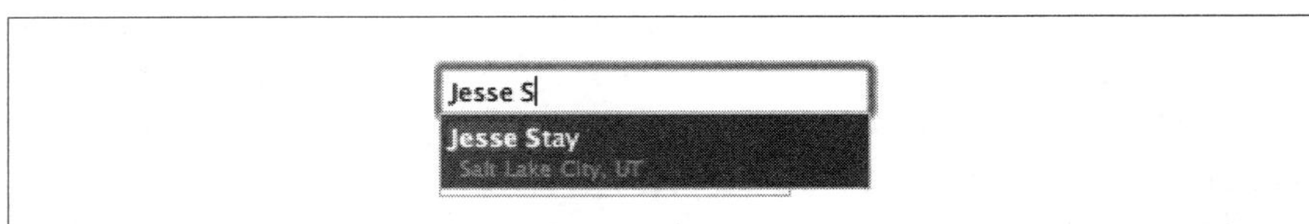

Figure 3-37. The result of our <fb:friend-selector/> example if I start typing "Jesse Stay"

Additional Information

- If a value that doesn't exist in the list is entered, `idname` becomes blank and the name value becomes that which was entered.
- If blank, the `idname` hidden field is not rendered.

<fb:multi-friend-input/>

`<fb:multi-friend-input/>`

Renders a form input text box that produces a drop-down list of suggestions for friends as the user types. The difference between this tag and the `<fb:friend-input/>` tag is that this one allows the user to select multiple friends. The tag produces an array in the POST variables with a list of user IDs that the user selected. The submitted form returns an `Array` of `id[ ]` variables.

FBML-Specific Attributes

Required

None.

Optional

`width=[string] default: 350px`
: The width of the field.

`border_color=[string] default: #8496ba`
: The color of the border.

`include_me=[true|false] default: false`
: If `true`, includes the logged-in user in the list of friends from which to select.

`max=[int] default: 20`
: The maximum number of friends that can be selected.

`exclude_ids=[array] default: none`
: A comma-separated list of friends to be excluded from the list. This can be useful when used within `<fb:request-form/>` tags to exclude users who have been invited.

`prefill_ids=[array] default: none`
: A comma-separated list of friends to include as already selected in the selector when the page loads. This cannot be used in `<fb:request-form/>` tags.

`prefill_locked=[true|false] default: false`
: When `true`, prevents editing of the preselected `prefill_ids` IDs. The user also cannot add other users.

Example FBML

Here is example FBML code for `<fb:multi-friend-input/>`:

```
<form>
<fb:multi-friend-input width="400px" border_color="#000"
    include_me="true" max="30" exclude_ids="4,1,2,3"
```

```
    prefill_ids="683545112"/>
</form>
```

Rendered HTML for Single Instance of Tag

The underlying HTML when rendered looks like this (Figure 3-38 shows the result):

```
<form>
  <input type="hidden" name="fb_sig_time" value="1206158663.8048" />
  <input type="hidden" name="fb_sig_added" value="0" />
  <input type="hidden" name="fb_sig_user" value="683545112" />
  <input type="hidden" name="fb_sig_profile_update_time"
      value="1205994295" />
  <input type="hidden" name="fb_sig_session_key"
      value="54aeab3103ef387539a31aa1-683545112" />
  <input type="hidden" name="fb_sig_expires" value="0" />
  <input type="hidden" name="fb_sig_api_key"
      value="ba19d367e2d8c4ea5813d54f2cbba136" />
  <input type="hidden" name="fb_sig"
      value="942c93c1b92f36b878b3dbe2c46ea16f" />
  <div style="padding-right:3px; width:400px;border:1px solid #000"
      class="clearfix">
    <div tabindex="-1" id="ids" class="clearfix tokenizer">
      <span class="tokenizer_stretcher">^_^</span>
      <span class="tab_stop"><input type="text" /></span>
    </div>
    <script type="text/javascript">
      onloadRegister(
        function() {
          var typeahead_source_instance2=new friend_source(
            '683545112-1206123558-1&u=683545112&include_me=1'
          );
          typeahead_source_instance2.set_exclude_ids(
            {"4":true,"1":true,"2":true,"3":true});
          var tok = new tokenizer(
            ge('ids'), typeahead_source_instance2,true,30);
          new token(
            {i:'683545112',t:'Jesse Stay',np:true}, tok);
          (new Image()).src='http://static.ak.facebook.com/inbox/images/
               token.gif';(
            new Image()).src='http://static.ak.facebook.com/inbox/images/
                 token_selected.gif';(
              new Image()).src='http://static.ak.facebook.com/inbox/
                   images/token_hover.gif';(
                new Image()).src='http://static.ak.facebook.com/inbox/
                     images/token_x.gif';})
      </script>
  </div>
</form>
```

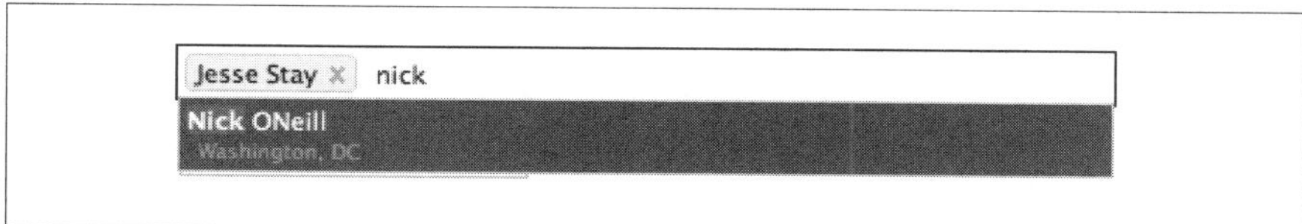

Figure 3-38. The result of our <fb:multi-friend-input/> example

Additional Information

- When used in a Mock AJAX form, only the last ID in the `Array` of `id[ ]` variables gets returned.
- This tag disables the friend input box when used on the same page as an `<fb:share-button/>` tag.
- Only one of these tags can be used on a page.

Dialog Boxes in Facebook—The Facebook "Pop Up"

Facebook itself does not support pop ups for applications. Facebook has, however, provided "dialog boxes" that appear as an overlay over the rest of the page. In this section we'll discuss the different tags that render these boxes.

<fb:dialog/>

```
<fb:dialog id="...">...<fb:dialog-content>...</fb:dialog-content></fb:dialog>
```

Creates an AJAX-based, pop-up dialog box that appears when a specified element on the page is clicked. The dialog box can contain any specified content, and uses Mock AJAX to refresh itself with new content.

FBML-Specific Attributes

Required

`id=[`*`string`*`] default: none`
: The ID of the dialog box. When an element that has the `clicktoshowdialog` attribute is clicked, this tag looks for this ID and displays the dialog box if the IDs are equal.

Optional

`cancel_button=[true|false] default: false`
: If `true`, displays a cancel button in the dialog box.

Required included tags

- `<fb:dialog-content/>`, described later in this chapter.

Optional included tags

- `<fb:dialog-title/>`, described later in this chapter.
- `<fb:dialog-button/>`, described later in this chapter.

Example FBML

The following `<fb:dialog/>` instance launches a dialog box on the submission of a form that has two buttons:

```
<fb:dialog id="my_dialog" cancel_button="true">
  <fb:dialog-content>Do you want to go to my blog?</fb:dialog-content>
  <fb:dialog-title>This is the &lt;fb:dialog/&gt; box.</fb:dialog-title>
  <fb:dialog-button type="button" value="Yes" href="http://staynalive.com"/>
  <fb:dialog-button type="button" value="No"
      href="http://apps.facebook.com/fbmlessentials"/>
</fb:dialog>
<p><a href="#" clicktoshowdialog="my_dialog">Click here to display the
    dialog...</a></p>
```

Rendered HTML for Single Instance of Tag

When you click the link shown in Figure 3-39...

Click here to display the dialog...

Figure 3-39. The link that results from our <fb:dialog/> example

...the dialog box shown in Figure 3-40 pops up on the page.

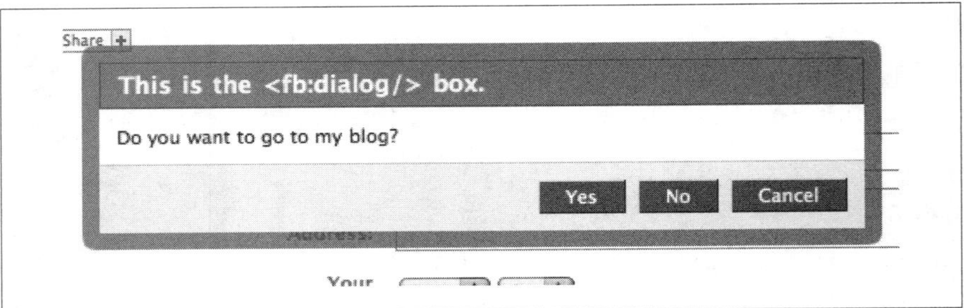

Figure 3-40. The dialog box

Additional Information

- For more flexibility in producing dialog boxes in Facebook, use the `Dialog` class in FBJS (see the "Dialogs" section in Chapter 4).
- See the `<fb:dialogresponse/>` tag for posting information from the submitted dialog back into the same dialog box (i.e., you want to keep the dialog box open but show new information based on what the user clicks).
- This tag is in beta at the time of this writing.

<fb:dialog-content/>

```
<fb:dialog-content>...</fb:dialog-content>
```

The content to display in the `<fb:dialog/>` box. It can be any type of HTML or FBML content.

FBML-Specific Attributes

Required

None.

Optional

None.

Example FBML

Please see `<fb:dialog/>` earlier in this chapter for an example of how to use this tag.

Additional Information

- This tag must be used inside `<fb:dialog/>` tags.

<fb:dialog-title/>

```
<fb:dialog-title>...</fb:dialog-title>
```

The title of the `<fb:dialog/>` box.

FBML-Specific Attributes

Required

None.

Optional

None.

Example FBML

Please see `<fb:dialog/>` earlier in this chapter for an example of how to use this tag.

Additional Information

- This tag must be used inside `<fb:dialog/>` tags.

<fb:dialog-button/>

```
<fb:dialog-button type="..." value="..."/>
```

Renders various types of buttons within `<fb:dialog/>` tags. Must be contained inside `<fb:dialog/>` tags.

FBML-Specific Attributes

Required

`type=[button|submit] default: none`
: The type of button to display. `button` displays a normal Facebook blue button. `submit` displays a standard submit button. Note that if you don't specify anything, the button will not be rendered.

`value=[`*`string`*`] default: none`
: The text to display inside the button.

Optional

`close_dialog=[true|false] default: true`
: If `true`, closes the dialog when the user clicks the button.

`href=[`*`string`*`] default: none`
: The URL to take the user to after clicking the button.

`form_id=[`*`string`*`] default: none`
: The ID of the form to submit when the button is clicked.

`clickrewriteurl=[`*`string`*`] default: none`
: See the section on "Mock AJAX" later in this chapter for more information on this attribute.

`clickrewriteid=[`*`string`*`] default: none`
: See the section on "Mock AJAX" later in this chapter for more information on this attribute.

`clickrewriteform=[string] default: none`
: See the section on "Mock AJAX" later in this chapter for more information on this attribute.

Example FBML

Please see the `<fb:dialog/>` tag earlier in this chapter for context.

Here are examples of the two different button types that can be created with `<fb:dialog-button/>`. The first is a normal Facebook blue button:

```
<fb:dialog-button type="button" value="Yes"/>
```

And the second is a standard submit button:

```
<fb:dialog-button type="submit" value="No"/>
```

Rendered HTML for Single Instance of Tag

The two buttons look exactly the same, but the HTML differs. To show you the difference, here is an `<input/>` tag with a `button` type:

```
<input class="inputsubmit" name="confirm" type="button" value="Yes"
  onclick="document.location='http://staynalive.com'" />
```

And here is an `<input/>` tag with a `submit` type:

```
<input class="inputsubmit" name="confirm" type="submit" value="No"
  onclick="document.location='http://apps.facebook.com/fbmlessentials'" />
```

Additional Information

- Multiple buttons can exist in one set of `<fb:dialog/>` tags.
- This tag must be used within `<fb:dialog/>` tags.

<fb:dialogresponse/>

```
<fb:dialogresponse>...<fb:dialog-content>...</fb:dialog-content>
    </fb:dialogresponse>
```

See the `<fb:dialog/>` tag earlier in this chapter for attributes and uses of `<fb:dialogresponse/>`. This tag takes all the same internal tags that an `<fb:dialog/>` box allows, and it also wraps around any response to a Mock AJAX call within an `<fb:dialog/>` box.

FBML-Specific Attributes

Required

None.

Optional

None.

Example FBML

Let's take our example from the `<fb:dialog/>` section and apply some Mock AJAX attributes to it. Here is the `<fb:dialog/>` call we used earlier, but with Mock AJAX attributes added in the `No` button:

```
<fb:dialog id="my_dialog" cancel_button="true">
  <fb:dialog-content><form id="my_form">Do you want to go to my blog?
      </form></fb:dialog-content>
  <fb:dialog-title>This is the &lt;fb:dialog/&gt; box.</fb:dialog-title>
  <fb:dialog-button type="button" value="Yes"
      href="http://staynalive.com"/>
  <fb:dialog-button type="button" value="No"
    clickrewriteurl="http://apps.facebook.com/fbmlessentials/
      get_dialog.php" click_rewrite_id="my_dialog"
    clickrewriteform="my_form"/>
</fb:dialog>
<p><a href="#" clicktoshowdialog="my_dialog">Click here to display
    the dialog... </a></p>
```

The data returned by `get_dialog.php` will need to be wrapped in `<fb:dialogresponse/>` tags like this:

```
<fb:dialogresponse>
  <fb:dialog-title>Response Title</fb:dialog-title>
  <fb:dialog-content>Response Content</fb:dialog-content>
  <fb:dialog-button type="button" value="Close"/>
</fb:dialogresponse>
```

Embedding Media With FBML

<fb:photo/>

`<fb:photo pid="..."/>`

Renders a Facebook photo based on the photo ID passed to it.

FBML-Specific Attributes

Required

`pid=[`*`int`*`] default: none`
: The Facebook ID of the photo.

Optional

`uid=[int] default: none`
: When the `pid` is not supplied by the API, this is the user ID used to find the `pid`.

`size=[thumb|small|normal|square|t|s|n|q] default: normal`
: The size to display the photo. Options are `t=thumb`, `s=small`, `n=normal`, and `q=square`.

`align=[left|right] default: left`
: The alignment of the photo.

Example FBML

The following FBML code takes a photo with a `pid` of 12345 for the user with an ID of 4 (Mark Zuckerberg) and displays it right-aligned as a square:

```
<fb:photo pid="12345" uid="4" size="square" align="right"/>
```

Additional Information

- When using a `pid` returned by the API or Facebook Query Language (FQL), do not supply the `uid` attribute.
- Be sure to wrap any data you want to display with the photo in `<fb:if-can-see-photo/>` tags.

<fb:mp3/>

```
<fb:mp3 src="..."/>
```

Need a playlist for your band? Want to allow your application's users to display their favorite music on their profile? This is a great tool for accomplishing these things and more. `<fb:mp3/>` displays a simple play button/music player for a specified MP3 file on your servers.

FBML-Specific Attributes

Required

`src=[string] default: none`
: The URL and path of the MP3 file on your servers. The URL must be absolute.

Optional

`title=[string] default: none`
: The title of the song.

`artist=[string]` default: none
: The name of the artist.

`album=[string]` default: none
: The name of the album.

`width=[int]` default: 300
: The width of the player, in pixels.

`height=[int]` default: 29
: The height of the player, in pixels.

Example FBML

Here is example FBML code for the `<fb:mp3/>` tag:

```
<fb:mp3 src="http://fbmlessentials.staynalive.com/metzener.mp3"
    title="Take on Me" artist="Metzener" album="Take on Me Single"/>
```

Rendered HTML for Single Instance of Tag

When you run the example and the page loads, an image appears, as shown in Figure 3-41.

Figure 3-41. The play button that results from our <fb:mp3/> example

When you click on the image, it starts playing, as shown in Figure 3-42.

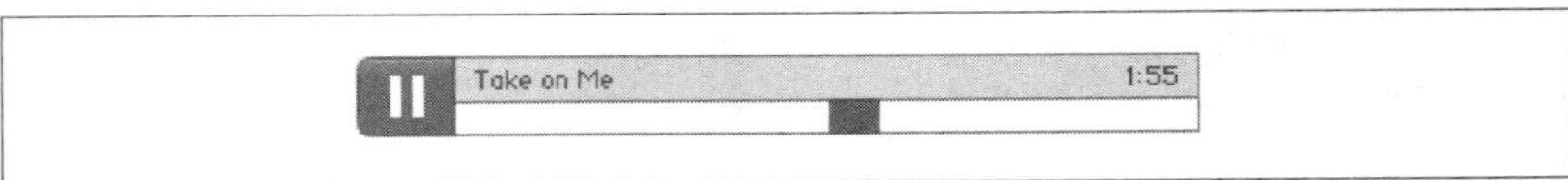

Figure 3-42. After clicking on the play button

Additional Information

- The file must end in the extension *.mp3*. Query strings and generic paths that still load an MP3 file will not work.
- Only *.mp3* files are supported.
- The file's bit rate must be in increments of 11 KHz.
- Nonstandard character sets will not work for the artist, title, or album.

<fb:swf/>

```
<fb:swf swfsrc="..."/>
```

Renders a standard SWF (Shockwave Flash) object. On profile pages, an image must be specified, and it will be displayed until the user clicks on it. On canvas pages, the SWF file works as normal.

FBML-Specific Attributes

Required

`swfsrc=[string] default: none`
: The URL of the Flash object. Must be an absolute URL.

Optional

`imgsrc=[string] default: http://static.ak.facebook.com/images/spacer.gif`
: The URL of an image to display when the page loads. This is useful in particular for the profile page, as an image must be displayed until the user clicks on it. This must be either a *.gif* or *.jpg* image.

`height=[int] default: none`
: The height of the image and the Flash object.

`width=[int] default: none`
: The width of the image and the Flash object.

`imgstyle=[string] default: none`
: The `style` attribute of the `<img/>` tag.

`imgclass=[string] default: none`
: The `class` attribute of the `<img/>` tag.

`flashvars=[string] default: none`
: URL-encoded Flash variables. Also sends the `fb_` values mentioned earlier in the section "Forms in FBML" in Chapter 2.

`swfbgcolor=[string] default: none`
: The background color of the Flash object.

`waitforclick=[true|false] default: true`
: If `false`, the Flash object autoplays. This works only on canvas pages.

`salign=[string] default: none`
: The `salign` attribute in the `<embed/>` tag.

`loop=[true|false] default: false`
: If `true`, loops the Flash object over and over.

quality=[high|medium|low] default: none
: The quality of the Flash object.

scale=[*string*] default: none
: The scaling to apply to the Flash object.

align=[left|center|right] default: none
: Describes how to align the Flash object.

wmode=[transparent|opaque|window] default: transparent
: The opacity of the Flash object.

Example FBML

I use the following <fb:swf/> example in my GrandCentral app[*] on Facebook:

```
<fb:swf imgsrc="http://grandcentral.jessestay.com/images/webbutton_01.jpg"
    swfsrc="http://embed.grandcentral.com/webcall/
    3f09cc369b1816d0990c5b125eb76374" width="227" swfbgcolor="#ffffff"
    height="93" waitforclick="false"/>
```

Rendered HTML for Single Instance of Tag

The converted SWF object in HTML looks like this (Figure 3-43 shows the result):

```
<div id="2413262772_fbswf_47e5dd74885221322368475" height="93" width="227"
    overflow="hidden">
</div>
<script type="text/javascript">
  swf_47e5dd74894734870324870 =
    new SWFObject(
      "http://embed.grandcentral.com/webcall/
          3f09cc369b1816d0990c5b125eb76374",
      "swf_47e5dd74894734870324870", "227", "93", "5.0.0", "#ffffff"
    );
  swf_47e5dd74894734870324870.addParam("allowScriptAccess", "never");
  swf_47e5dd74894734870324870.addParam("wmode", "transparent");
  swf_47e5dd74894734870324870.addVariable("fb_local_connection",
      "_id_47e5dd748843e6a84442969");
  swf_47e5dd74894734870324870.addVariable("fb_sig_time", "1206246772.5586");
  swf_47e5dd74894734870324870.addVariable("fb_sig_added", "1");
  swf_47e5dd74894734870324870.addVariable("fb_sig_user", "683545112");
  swf_47e5dd74894734870324870.addVariable("fb_sig_profile_update_time",
      "1205994295");
  swf_47e5dd74894734870324870.addVariable("fb_sig_session_key",
      "5e34a2335cf43f2b46ddb770-683545112");
  swf_47e5dd74894734870324870.addVariable("fb_sig_expires", "0");
  swf_47e5dd74894734870324870.addVariable("fb_sig_api_key",
      "a5438e29c1b4df4ec650d374b4175741");
  swf_47e5dd74894734870324870.addVariable("fb_sig",
      "ee27f0b9b9859a998e7c237ab4c4aec6");
  swf_47e5dd74894734870324870.addVariable("string_table",
```

[*] See *http://www.facebook.com/apps/application.php?id=2413262772*.

```
        "/js_strings.php/t83767/en_US");
    swf_47e5dd74894734870324870.addVariable("swf_id",
        "swf_47e5dd74894734870324870");
    swf_47e5dd74894734870324870.fallback_js_fcn = spawn_flash_update_dialog;
    swf_47e5dd74894734870324870.fallback_html =
        "\x3cdiv class=\x22flash_fallback\x22\x3e\x3cdiv
      class=\x22flash_fallback_border\x22\x3e\x3cdiv class=
          \x22flash_fallback_header\x22\x3eFlash
      Player upgrade required\x3c/div\x3e\x3cdiv class=\x22flash_fallback_
          explanation\x22
      id=\x22flash_fallback_47e5dd74896126656860712\x22\x3eYou must download
          and install the latest version of the Adobe Flash Player to view
          this content.\x3c/div\x3e\x3cdiv class=\x22flash_fallback_button\
          x22\x3e\x3cinput type=\x22button\x22 class=\x22inputbutton\x22
          onclick=\x22this.disabled=true;getFlashPlayer();\x22 id=\x22\x22
          name=\x22\x22 value=\x22Download Flash\x22 /
          \x3e\x3c/div\x3e\x3c/div\x3e\x3c/div\x3e";
    swf_47e5dd74894734870324870.write("2413262772_fbswf_
        47e5dd74885221322368475");
</script>
```

Figure 3-43. Our <fb:swf/> example produces this "Call Me!" button

Additional Information

- As well as the traditional POST variables (discussed in Chapter 2) that get passed to the SWF when it is loaded, Facebook also passes `allowScriptAccess="never"` to the SWF.
- Facebook requires Flash 9.0 for all SWFs.
- The `flashvars` attribute must be entirely lowercase.
- Keep in mind that the Flash object is contained in `<div/>` tags. This could affect the `display` styles of the object.

<fb:flv/>

```
<fb:flv src="..."/>
```

Renders a Flash-based FLV (Flash Video) player that can play FLV audio or video files.

FBML-Specific Attributes

Required

`src=[string] default: none`
: The URL of the FLV file. This must be an absolute URL and must be FLV-encoded.

Optional

`height=[int] default: none`
: The height of the FLV. This must be specified if using Internet Explorer.

`width=[int] default: none`
: The width of the FLV. This must be specified if using Internet Explorer.

`title=[string] default: none`
: The title of the audio or video.

Example FBML

Here is example FBML code for the `<fb:flv/>` tag:

```
<fb:flv src="http://fbmlessentials.staynalive.com/curtainLoop.flv"
    width="400" height="400" title="Curtain Loop from
    http://theflashblog.com/?p=86"/>
```

Rendered HTML for Single Instance of Tag

The source HTML of the rendered object looks like this (Figures 3-44 and 3-45 show the results):

```
<div class="swf_holder" id="holder_fb_flv47e5e182263d28c68824513"></div>
<script type="text/javascript">
  so_fb_flv47e5e182263d28c68824513_47e5e182291b47871811755 =
    new SWFObject("http://static.ak.facebook.com/swf/flv_ad.swf?58:55325",
    "so_fb_flv47e5e182263d28c68824513_47e5e182291b47871811755", "400",
        "400", "5.0.0", "#000000");
  so_fb_flv47e5e182263d28c68824513_47e5e182291b47871811755.addParam
      ("wmode", "transparent");
  so_fb_flv47e5e182263d28c68824513_47e5e182291b47871811755.addVariable
      ("video_src",
    "http%3A%2F%2Ffbmlessentials.staynalive.com%2FcurtainLoop.flv");
  so_fb_flv47e5e182263d28c68824513_47e5e182291b47871811755.addVariable
      ("deblocking", "1");
  so_fb_flv47e5e182263d28c68824513_47e5e182291b47871811755.addVariable
      ("video_title",
    "Curtain+Loop+from+http%3A%2F%2Ftheflashblog.com%2F%3Fp%3D86");
  so_fb_flv47e5e182263d28c68824513_47e5e182291b47871811755.addVariable
      ("scale_thumb", "0");
  so_fb_flv47e5e182263d28c68824513_47e5e182291b47871811755.addVariable
      ("keep_last_frame", "1");
  so_fb_flv47e5e182263d28c68824513_47e5e182291b47871811755.addVariable
      ("show_controls", "1");
```

```
    so_fb_flv47e5e182263d28c68824513_47e5e182291b47871811755.addVariable
        ("string_table",
      "/js_strings.php/t83767/en_US");
    so_fb_flv47e5e182263d28c68824513_47e5e182291b47871811755.addVariable
        ("swf_id",
      "so_fb_flv47e5e182263d28c68824513_47e5e182291b47871811755");
    so_fb_flv47e5e182263d28c68824513_47e5e182291b47871811755.fallback_js
        _fcn = spawn_flash_update_dialog;
    so_fb_flv47e5e182263d28c68824513_47e5e182291b47871811755.fallback_
        html = "\x3cdiv class=\x22flash_fallback\x22\x3e\x3cdiv
          class=\x22flash_fallback_border\x22\x3e\x3cdiv
      class=\x22flash_fallback_header\x22\x3eFlash Player upgrade
      required\x3c/div\x3e\x3cdiv class=\x22flash_fallback_explanation\x22
      id=\x22flash_fallback_47e5e1822926f7b33344160\x22\x3eYou must download
      and install the latest version of the Adobe Flash Player to view this
      content.\x3c/div\x3e\x3cdiv class=\x22flash_fallback_button\x22\x3e\
      x3cinput type=\x22button\x22 class=\x22inputbutton\x22 onclick=\
      x22this.disabled=true;getFlashPlayer();\x22 id=\x22\x22 name=\x22\x22
      value=\x22Download Flash\x22 /\x3e\x3c/div\x3e\x3c/div\x3e\x3c/div\
      x3e";
    so_fb_flv47e5e182263d28c68824513_47e5e182291b47871811755.write
        ("holder_fb_flv47e5e182263d28c68824513");
</script>
```

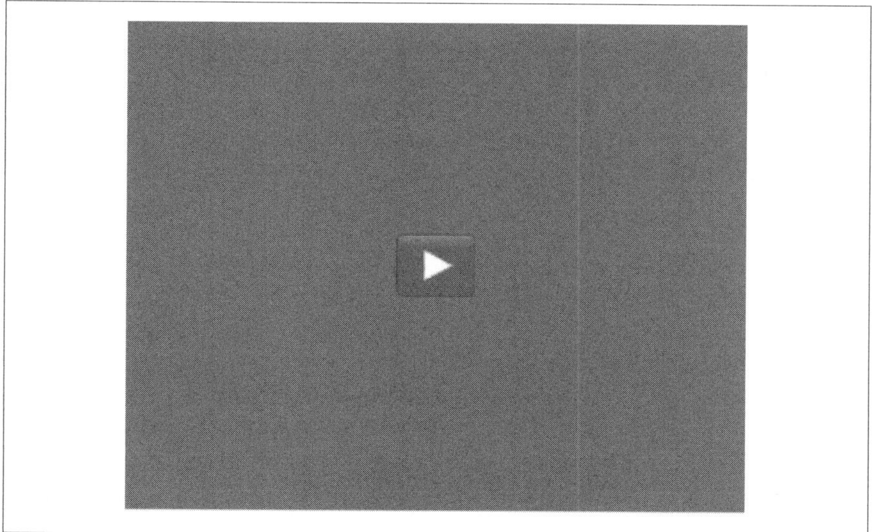

Figure 3-44. The result of our <fb:flv/> example when the page is loading

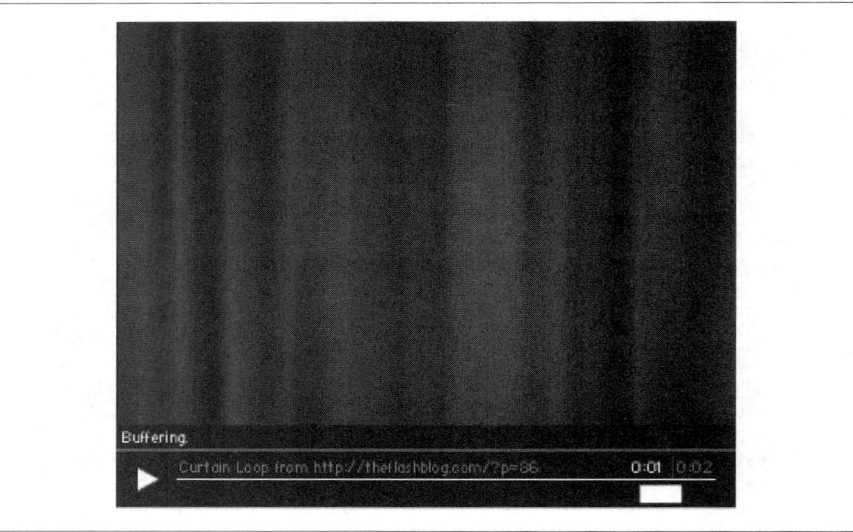

Figure 3-45. The result of our <fb:flv/> example when the play button is clicked

<fb:silverlight/>

```
<fb:silverlight silverlightsrc="..."/>
```

Renders a Microsoft Silverlight control. At the time of this writing, this tag is not yet functional.

FBML-Specific Attributes

Required

`silverlightsrc=[string] default: none`
: The source URL for your Silverlight code.

Optional

`imgsrc=[string] default: http://static.ak.facebook.com/images/spacer.gif`
: The source of an image to display; requires a user to click to activate the control. This is required on profile pages to prevent clutter.

`height=[int] default: none`
: The height of the image or Silverlight object.

`width=[int] default: none`
: The width of the image or Silverlight object.

`imgstyle=[string] default: none`
: The `<img/>` `style` attribute for use with the `imgsrc` attribute.

`imgclass=[string] default: none`
: The `<img/>` `class` attribute for use with the `imgsrc` attribute.

`swfbgcolor=[string] default: none`
: The background color of the Silverlight control.

Virally Promoting Your App With FBML

The following section describes several tags that you can use to virally promote your application. One of the strengths of Facebook is the rich access it provides to friends lists, and the tools it offers for promoting applications through those friends. As an application developer, with just knowledge of FBML you can do many things to spread your app to others on Facebook very quickly.

Request and Notification Tags

Notification tags require some API knowledge and access, but as you saw in the "Hello Friends" example in Chapter 1, with request tags you can create simple invite forms using just a series of FBML tags.

<fb:notif-subject/>

`<fb:notif-subject>...</fb:notif-subject>`

Specifies the subject of an email sent using the `notifications.send()` API method. This FBML works only within that FBML call.

FBML-Specific Attributes

Required

None.

Optional

None.

Example FBML

Send the following FBML code in a `notifications.send()` API call:

```
<fb:notif-subject>This is the subject of the E-mail</fb:notif-subject>
```

<fb:notif-page/>

`<fb:notif-page>...</fb:notif-page>`

Specifies the content of the notification, displayed on a user's notifications page. It works only from within a `notifications.send()` API method call.

FBML-Specific Attributes

Required

None.

Optional

None.

Example FBML

Send the following FBML code in a `notifications.send()` API call:

```
<fb:notif-page>Add the <a href="http://apps.facebook.com/fbmlessentials">
FBML Essentials app!
</a></fb:notif-page>
```

<fb:notif-email/>

`<fb:notif-email>...</fb:notif-email>`

Specifies the content of the email to be sent to the user in a `notifications.send()` API method call. It can be used only in the `notifications.send()` API call. This is a great way to send an email to the user (not the user's Facebook inbox, but the user's real email address) and parse FBML beforehand as part of the email.

FBML-Specific Attributes

Required

None.

Optional

None.

Example FBML

To specify the FBML to be parsed for the user, send the following in a `notifications.send()` API call:

```
<fb:notif-email>
Dear <fb:name uid="4"/>,
```

```
Nice Profile!

-Jesse
</fb:notif-email>
```

<fb:request-form/>

```
<fb:request-form type="..." content="...">...</fb:request-form>
```

Renders a standard Facebook invite form. It must include either an `<fb:multi-friend-selector/>` tag or a combination of `<fb:multi-friend-input/>` or `<fb:friend-selector/>` tags and the `<fb:request-form-submit/>` tag. FBML invite tags are one of the biggest reasons to base your application on FBML instead of purely on `<iframe/>` tags, as these invite tags can save developers a lot of time producing a list of friends and necessary calls to invite those friends. It should also be noted that FBML is the most effective method of sending invites—these forms are the only ways to invite a user's friends to an app. To display a custom form on your own, you may want to look into the `notifications` API call.

FBML-Specific Attributes

Required

`type=[`*`string`*`] default: none`
: The name to include in the invite. It will appear as something to the effect of "1 [*type*] request" under "Requests" in the upper-right corner of your main Facebook page. It has a limit of 20 characters.

`content=[`*`string`*`] default: none`
: The content of the request invitation to send to the friend(s) being invited.

Optional

`invite=[true|false] default: false`
: Specifies whether it is an invitation or a request. The only difference is that if `true`, it says, "`[`*`name`*`] sent an invitation using [`*`type`*`]:`" whereas if `false`, it says, "`[`*`name`*`] sent a request using [`*`type`*`]`:".

`action=[`*`string`*`] default: http://apps.facebook.com/yourapp/null`
: The URL to redirect the user after they submit the form, or after they click "Skip" in the form.

`method=[GET|POST] default: POST`
: Specifies whether to submit the form via either the method GET or POST.

Example FBML

The following FBML example for the <fb:request-form/> tag comes from our "Hello Friends" example in Chapter 1:

```
<fb:request-form action="index.php" method="POST" invite="true"
    type="FBML Essentials" content="Hello Friend. <fb:req-choice
    url='http://apps.facebook.com/fbmlessentials' label='Go there!'/>">
  <fb:multi-friend-selector showborder="false"
      actiontext="Invite your friends to use FBML Essentials.">
</fb:request-form>
```

Here's another example, this time using <fb:multi-friend-input/> and <fb:request-form-submit/>:

```
<fb:request-form action="index.php" method="POST" invite="true"
    type="FBML Essentials" content="Hello Friend. <fb:req-choice
    url='http://apps.facebook.com/fbmlessentials' label='Go there!'/>">
  <fb:multi-friend-input width="350px" border_color="#8496ba"
      exclude_ids="4,5,10,15" />
  <fb:request-form-submit/>
</fb:request-form>
```

Rendered HTML for Single Instance of Tag

The first <fb:request-form/> example renders as shown in Figure 3-46.

The second <fb:request-form/> example renders as shown in Figure 3-47.

Additional Information

- <fb:request-form/> returns an `ids[ ]` attribute with a comma-separated list of IDs that the invite was sent to. This attribute gets passed to the `action` attribute specified in the <fb:request-form/>.

<fb:multi-friend-selector/>

```
<fb:multi-friend-selector actiontext="..."/>
```

Renders a full-page friend selector with pictures of all of the user's friends and their names and networks. This control handles all limits that Facebook enforces on applications, preventing the user from going over their allocated number of requests per day for your application. For a smaller version of this without the pictures, see the condensed version of <fb:multi-friend-selector/>. This tag can be used only within <fb:request-form/> tags. Use the `condensed` attribute to produce a smaller version of this.

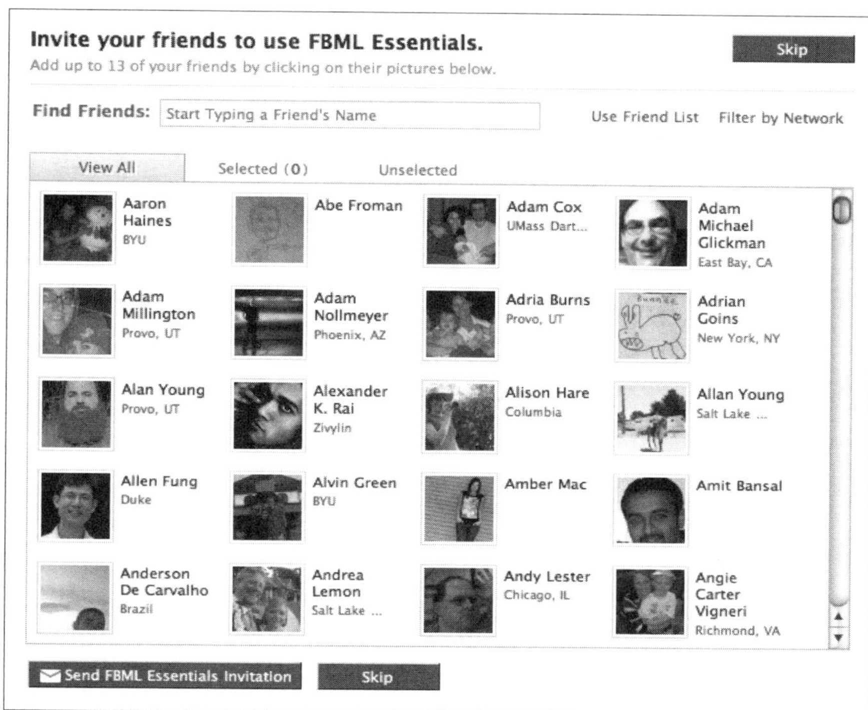

Figure 3-46. The result of our first <fb:request-form/> example (using <fb:multi-friend-selector/>)

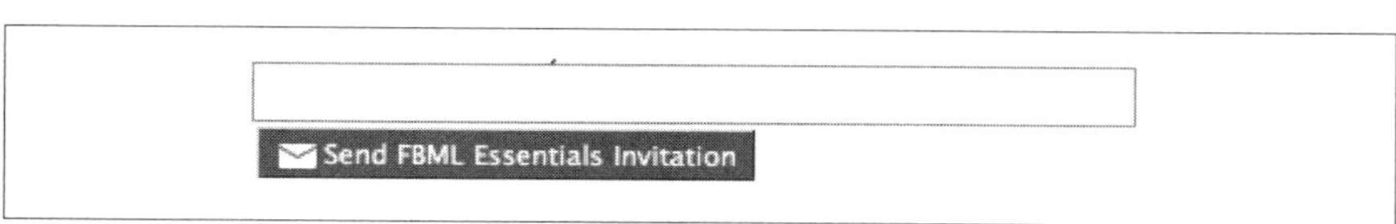

Figure 3-47. The result of our second <fb:request-form/> example (using <fb:multi-friend-input/>)

FBML-Specific Attributes

Required

`actiontext=[`*`string`*`] default: none`
: The invite text to include in the multi-friend selector.

Optional

`condensed=[true|false] default: false`
: If `true`, shows the condensed form of `<fb:multi-friend-selector/>`.

showborder=[true|false] default: false
: If true, displays a border around the multi-friend selector. Works only if condensed="false".

rows=[*int*] default: 5
: The number of rows of friends to display. Works only if condensed="false".

max=[1...35] default: none
: The maximum number of friends allowed to be selected. This caps at the number of invites allowed to your app at a given time that remain for that user.

exclude_ids=[*array*] default: none
: A comma-separated list of friends to be excluded from the list of friends.

bypass=[step|cancel|skip] default: skip
: Each multi-friend selector includes a bypass button. This attribute designates the kind of bypass button to be used: step renders "Skip This Step"; cancel renders "Cancel"; and skip renders "Skip." Works only if condensed="false".

unselected_rows=[4...15] default: 6
: The number of unselected rows to display in the condensed form of <fb:multi-friend-selector/>. Works only if condensed="true".

selected_rows=[0,5...15] default: 5
: The number of rows to display in the selected portion of the condensed form of <fb:multi-friend-selector/>. If 0, displays only a single box for both selected and unselected portions. Works only if condensed="true".

Example FBML

See the <fb:request-form/> tag earlier in this chapter for an example of the noncondensed <fb:multi-friend-selector/>.

Here is example FBML code for a condensed <fb:multi-friend-selector/> (Figure 3-48 shows the result):

```
<fb:request-form action="index.php" method="POST" invite="true"
     type="FBML Essentials" content="Hello Friend.">
  <fb:multi-friend-selector condensed="true" exclude_ids="1,4,5,6" />
  <fb:request-form-submit/>
</fb:request-form>
```

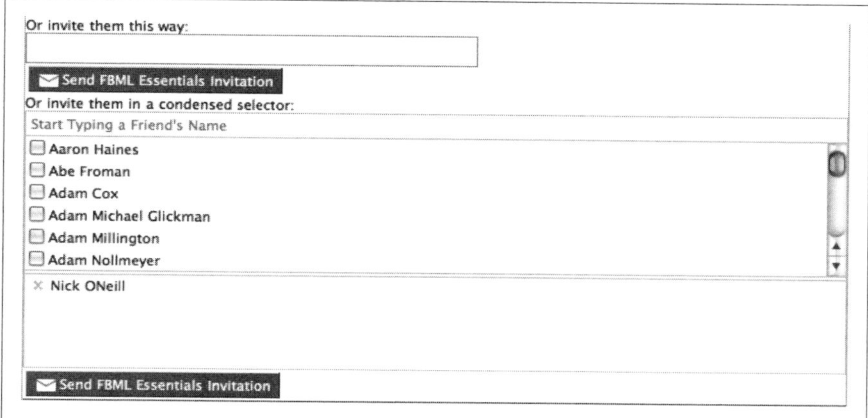

Figure 3-48. The result of our condensed <fb:multi-friend-selector/> example

Additional Information

- This tag can be used only in `<fb:request-form/>` tags.
- To use this tag for notifications, you have to generate your own HTML. View the source to see how Facebook does it, or create your own.

<fb:req-choice/>

```
<fb:req-choice url="..." label="..."/>
```

Provides a button to be used in the invite request sent to the user's friends.

FBML-Specific Attributes

Required

`url=[`*`string`*`] default: none`
: The URL to direct the user to when they click on the button. Must be an absolute URL.

`label=[`*`string`*`] default: none`
: Text to display on the button.

Optional

None.

Example FBML

Please see the `<fb:request-form/>` tag earlier in this chapter for an example of this tag.

Additional Information

- If two buttons with the same URL are used, only the last one will be rendered.
- Each request defaults to have one ignore button. Having more than one ignore button can cause problems.
- `<fb:req-choice/>` is built to be used within the `content` attribute of the `<fb:request-form/>`. Be sure to properly encode it to fit within the quotes of that attribute.
- You may have as many `<fb:req-choice/>` buttons as needed.

<fb:request-form-submit/>

```
<fb:request-form-submit/>
```

Creates a submit button for an `<fb:request-form/>`. When a `uid` is specified, this tag forces the form to be submitted to a specified user, if the button is clicked.

FBML-Specific Attributes

Required

None.

Optional

`uid=[`*`int`*`] default: none`
: The ID of the user to send the form to.

`label=[`*`text`*`] default: none`
: The text to include in the submit button, if `uid` is used. It must include either `%n` or `%N` in place of where the user's name will be in order to use it in this manner.

Example FBML

Please see the `<fb:request-form/>`tag earlier in this chapter for an example of this tag.

Feed Forms

Feed forms are another shortcut you can take for virally spreading your application. By adding a simple `fbtype` attribute to your form, Facebook will intercept your form submission and present the user with a dialog box that asks if the user would like to publish a news item to either their Mini-Feed or their friends' News Feeds. The code referenced in the `action` parameter of the form should return JSON data in the form of a News Feed template. The following is an example of the form you submit. Notice the `fbtype` attribute in the form (you can also see this in action in the FBML Essentials app on Facebook):

```
<form fbtype="feedStory" action=
        "http://fbmlessentials.staynalive.com/index.php">
    <input type="text" name="status"  value="" />
    <input type="hidden" name="submit" value="1" />
    <input type="hidden" name="action" value="feedforms" />
    <input type="hidden" name="notabs" value="true" />
    <input type="submit" value="Submit" name="submit"
        label="Publish This Story" />
</form>
```

The returning code in *http://fbmlessentials.staynalive.com/index.php?submit=1&action=feedforms¬abs=true* would return JSON data that looks like this:

```
{ 'method': 'feedStory',
  'content': {
    'next':
        'http://apps.facebook.com/fbmlessentials/index.php?action=feedforms',
    'feed': {
      'title_template': '{actor} published status',
      'title_data': { 'status': $_POST['status'] },
      'body_template': 'New status is "{status}"',
      'body_data': { 'status': $_POST['status'] }
    }
  }
}
```

The two variables that can be included in the `fbtype` attribute are `feedStory` and `multiFeedStory`. When `feedStory` is used, the form gets published to the user's Mini-Feed. When `multiFeedStory` is used, the form gets published to the user's friends' News Feeds. You can also use the `fbnext` attribute to specify a URL in case there is an error in the process of submitting the feed story.

Feed forms aren't the only way of posting to a user's News and Mini-Feeds, but it does guarantee better chances of your News Feed item appearing in the user's News or Mini-Feed when you get the user's permission first via the feed form. If your application can afford it, it is strongly suggested that you utilize feed forms to submit feed stories to your users and users' friends. Look at the example in the FBML Essentials application on Facebook to see this in action.

The Wall

Wall attachments, which users include in their Wall posts, can be another great way to virally promote your application. You'll especially want to check out the `<fb:attachment-preview/>` tag for some ways to do this. The tags in this section offer ways to create your own Walls within your Facebook application.

<fb:wall/>

```
<fb:wall>...</fb:wall>
```

Emulates the Wall widget seen on user profiles, allowing you to have Wall-like environments within your application. This can be a great way to add a messaging system within your application.

FBML-Specific Attributes

Required

None.

Optional

None.

Example FBML

Here is example FBML code for a simulated Wall using the `<fb:wall/>` tag (Figure 3-49 shows the result):

```
<fb:wall>
  <fb:wallpost t="1" uid="683545112">
    I agree Mark - F8 FTW!
    <fb:wallpost-action href="http://apps.facebook.com/fbmlessentials">
        Check out my new app!</fb:wallpost-action>
  </fb:wallpost>
  <fb:wallpost t="1" uid="4">Facebook Rocks!</fb:wallpost>
</fb:wall>
```

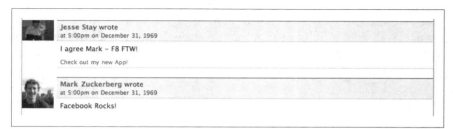

Figure 3-49. The result of our <fb:wall/> example

<fb:wallpost/>

```
<fb:wallpost uid="...">...</fb:wallpost>
```

Produces a Wall post within an `<fb:wall/>` tag. It is not required to be inside `<fb:wall/>` tags, however.

FBML-Specific Attributes

Required

`uid=[`*`int`*`] default: none`
: The user ID of the Facebook user who is making the post.

Optional

`t=[`*`int`*`] default: blank`
: Time, in epoch seconds, to be displayed in the Wall post. `1` is 5 p.m. on December 31, 1969. When blank, a date and time are not displayed.

Example FBML

Please see `<fb:wall/>` earlier in this chapter for an example of this tag.

<fb:wallpost-action/>

```
<fb:wallpost-action href="...">...</fb:wallpost-action>
```

Produces a link within `<fb:wallpost/>` tags for users to click on. This tag must be within `<fb:wallpost/>` tags.

FBML-Specific Attributes

Required

`href=[`*`string`*`] default: none`
: The URL of the link. This URL must be absolute.

Optional

None.

Example FBML

Please see `<fb:wall/>` earlier for an example of this tag.

<fb:attachment-preview/>

`<fb:attachment-preview>...</fb:attachment-preview>`

Provides a link to a Wall message or text that, when clicked, renders a preview of the attachment.

FBML-Specific Attributes

Required

None.

Optional

None.

Example FBML

The following FBML example renders a link that says, "Click here to preview the attachment for this message." When the user clicks on that link, a preview of the attachment appears:

```
<fb:attachment-preview>
Click here to preview the attachment for this message
</fb:attachment-preview>
```

Additional Information

- This tag is for use with display of Wall attachments. See the application setup to specify the URL that contains code to display the attachment.
- This tag cannot be used in an `<fb:wall/>` tag.

The <fb:add-section-button/> Tag

In early 2008, Facebook announced details of its plans to release a new design. As part of that design, it will release some new features into the API to give developers more integration points on their users' profiles. By the time you read this book, these changes will most likely be implemented.

One of the most notable features of the new API and design is the addition of the `<fb:add-section-button/>` FBML tag. This tag places a button in the app that, when clicked, allows the user to add an application to their profile's main page or to the "Info" tab introduced in the new profile design. We'll cover details of this tag in this section.

<fb:add-section-button/>

```
<fb:add-section-button "..."/>
```

Renders an "Add to Profile" or "Add to Info" button on an application's canvas page. After calling `profile.setFBML` or `profile.setInfo` on your app, this button allows you to add a profile box or additional information to the main profile area, to the "Boxes" tab, or to the "Info" tab. Where it appears partly depends on how you call `profile.setFBML`: if the `profile_main` parameter is set, it will appear on the main profile section of the user's profile; if not, it will appear under the "Boxes" tab. Where it appears also depends on the section you specify. If you specify a section of "Info," the information you set in the `profile.setInfo` API call will be sent to the user's "Info" tab. When you have called this once for the given section type, the button will no longer appear for that section type until the user removes it from his profile.

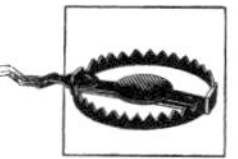

It is important to note that this tag is still under development at the time of this writing, so the way it works may change by the time you read this. Please refer to *http://wiki.developers.facebook.com/index.php/New_Design_Narrow_Boxes* and also to *http://wiki.developers.facebook.com/index.php/Fb:add-section-button* for more information about this tag. I will update this book's Facebook Page when this tag is updated.

FBML-Specific Attributes

Required

`section=[profile|info] default: none`
: The section in which to place the content specified in the `profile.setInfo` or `profile.setFBML` API calls.

Optional

None.

Example FBML

Here is example FBML code for the `<fb:add-section-button/>` tag:

```
<fb:add-section-button section="profile"/>
```

Rendered HTML for Single Instance of Tag

Assuming the user has not already clicked on the button for the profile section, the example FBML will render something that looks like Figure 3-50.

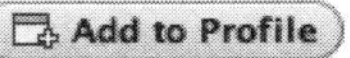

Figure 3-50. The "Add to Profile" button

Additional Information

- This tag works only on canvas pages.
- This tag is a work in progress at the time of this writing. Please refer to this book's Facebook Page to make sure you have the most up-to-date information.

Miscellaneous Tools for Rendering Data Using FBML

<fb:time/>

```
<fb:time t="..."/>
```

Renders the time to the user. You pass in a time and date, in epoch seconds, and it gives you a nicely formatted time. If the time you enter is the same day as the current day, only the time is displayed in `hour:minutes[am|pm]` format. If not the same day, but the same year, the year is not displayed, so the format is `Month Day hour:minutes[am|pm]`. If neither the same day nor year, it is displayed in `Month Day, Year hour:minutes[am|pm]` format.

FBML-Specific Attributes

Required

`t=[int] default: none`
: The time to display, in epoch seconds.

Optional

`tz=[string] default: the logged-in-user's time zone`
: The time zone to display. Accepted formats are PHP's list of supported time zones (see *http://us.php.net/manual/en/timezones.php*) and `+/-` formats such as `Etc/GMT-7`.

`preposition=[true|false] default: false`
: The preposition, as necessary, added to the date and time ("at," "on").

Example FBML

The following are some examples of the `<fb:time/>` tag and what they produce. This FBML code:

```
<fb:time t="1"/>
```

would produce this:

```
December 31, 1969 5:00pm
```

whereas this FBML code:

```
<fb:time t="1" tz="America/Boise" preposition="true"/>
```

would produce this:

```
5:00pm on December 31, 1969
```

<fb:fbmlversion/>

```
<fb:fbmlversion/>
```

Prints the version of FBML currently in scope. If used outside of `<fb:fbml/>` tags, prints the latest version of FBML.

FBML-Specific Attributes

Required

None.

Optional

None.

Example FBML

In the following example, the first instance of `<fb:fbmlversion/>` will print "1.0". The second will print "1.1", which is the current version of FBML at the time of this writing:

```
<fb:fbml version="1.0">
  The version listed here is <fb:fbmlversion/>
</fb:fbml>
The version listed here is <fb:fbmlversion/>
```

<fb:redirect/>

```
<fb:redirect url="..."/>
```

Redirects the page to the specified URL. This is the best way to redirect a user to a new page in a Facebook application canvas page.

FBML-Specific Attributes

Required

`url=[`*`string`*`] default: none`
: The URL to redirect the user to.

Optional

None.

Example FBML

To redirect the user to the FBML Essentials app home page, the `<fb:redirect/>` tag would look like this.

```
<fb:redirect url="http://apps.facebook.com/fbmlessentials"/>
```

<fb:board/>

`<fb:board xid="...">...</fb:board>`

Creates a discussion board, controlled by Facebook. The board's data is not accessible by any underlying server code of the programmer. When you specify an `xid` for the board, Facebook is able to track which topics and discussions go under which board.

FBML-Specific Attributes

Required

`xid=[`*`string`*`] default: none`
: The unique identifier for the board. Each board in your application should have its own identifier. Note that only alphanumeric (A–Z, a–z, 0–9), underscores (_), and hyphens (-) are allowed.

Optional

`canpost=[true|false] default: true`
: If `true`, the user viewing the page can post to the board.

`candelete=[true|false] default: false`
: If `true`, any user viewing the page can delete any topic or post to the board.

`canmark=[true|false] default: false`
: If `true`, any user viewing the page can mark a post as relevant or irrelevant.

`cancreatetopic=[true|false] default: true`
: If `true`, any user viewing the page can create a new topic.

`numtopics=[int] default: 3`
: The maximum number of topics to show in the first page of the board. Clicking on the "See All" link will still show all topics.

`callbackurl=[string] default: the current page`
: The reference point for all actions within the board. This is the URL to fetch configuration for the discussion board.

`returnurl=[string] default: the current page`
: The URL to take the user back to when they click on the "Return" link.

Example FBML

The following FBML code example produces two discussion boards using the `<fb:board/>` tag, both on the same page (Figure 3-51 shows the result):

```
<div style="width:300px">
<fb:board xid="discussion_board"
          canpost="true"
          candelete="false"
          canmark="false"
          cancreatetopic="true"
          numtopics="5"
          returnurl="http://apps.facebook.com/fbmlessentials/board.php">
   <fb:title>Discuss FBML Essentials</fb:title>
</fb:board>
</div>
<div style="width:300px">
<fb:board xid="discussion_board_2"
          canpost="true"
          candelete="false"
          canmark="false"
          cancreatetopic="true"
          numtopics="5"
          returnurl="http://apps.facebook.com/fbmlessentials/board.php">
   <fb:title>Discuss Facebook Trivia</fb:title>
</fb:board>
</div>
```

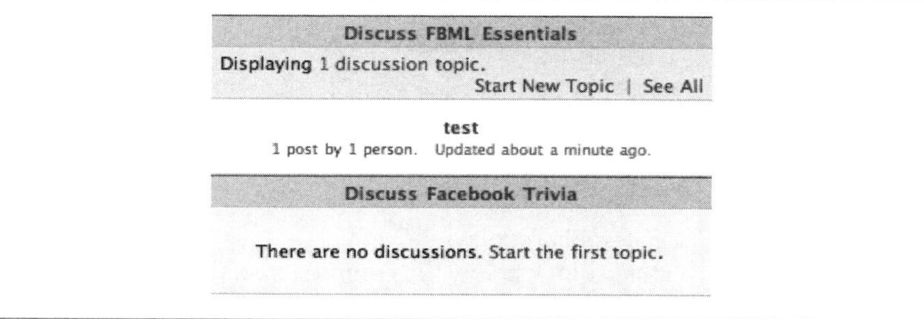

Figure 3-51. The resulting discussion boards from our <fb:board/> examples

Additional Information

- More than one `<fb:board/>` can exist on the same page, as long as the blocks have different `xids`.
- To display the `<fb:board/>` block at a certain width, wrap it in a `<div/>` block with a styled width.

<fb:comments/>

```
<fb:comments xid="..." canpost="..." candelete="..." numposts="...">...
    </fb:comments>
```

Similar to the `<fb:board/>` tag (described earlier in this chapter), this tag creates a Wall-like component that users can comment on. The data for these `<fb:comments/>` blocks is not available to the developer and is controlled by Facebook. It provides an easy way for your users to make comments.

FBML-Specific Attributes

Required

`xid=[`*`string`*`] default: none`
: The unique identifier for this comments block. Each post within the series of posting comments will reference this identifier.

`canpost=[true|false] default: none`
: If `true`, any viewing user can post to the comments.

`candelete=[true|false] default: none`
: If `true`, any viewing user can delete comments.

`numposts=[`*`int`*`] default: none`
: The total number of posts visible when the page loads. The "See All" link allows the user to still see all posts.

Optional

`callbackurl=[`*`string`*`] default:` *`the current page`*
: The URL that Facebook references to identify the source of the current comments block.

`returnurl=[`*`string`*`] default:` *`the current page`*
: The URL to take the user to after the user clicks the "Return" link.

`showform=[true|false] default: true`
: If `true`, shows the form block below the comments on the first page of the comments. The user will not have to click the "See All" link to add a comment this way.

`send_notification_id=[int] default: none`
: The ID of the user to send notifications to when comments are made for the current comment block.

Example FBML

The following example FBML generates a simple comments block for the "Hello Friends" example in Chapter 1 (Figure 3-52 shows the result):

```
<div style="width:300px">
<fb:comments xid="hello_friends_comments" canpost="true" candelete="false"
    returnurl="http://apps.facebook.com/fbmlessentials/">
  <fb:title>Comments for Hello Friends Example</fb:title>
</fb:comments>
</div>
```

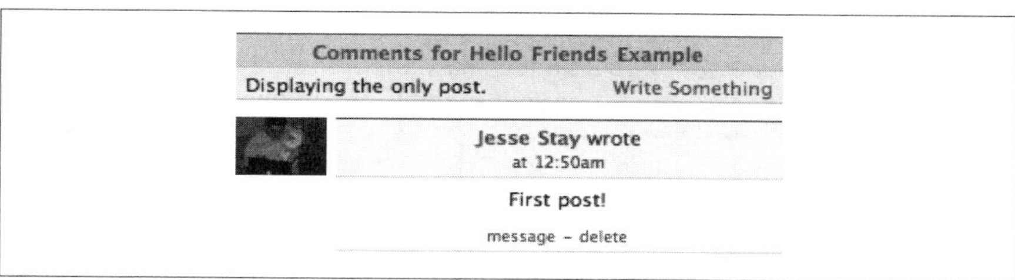

Figure 3-52. The resulting comments block from our <fb:comments/> example

Additional Information

- You can add more than one `<fb:comments/>` on a single page. Just specify different `xid`s for each `<fb:comments/>` block.
- To specify a width for your `<fb:comments/>` block, wrap it in a styled `<div/>`.

<fb:mobile/>

`<fb:mobile>...</fb:mobile>`

Displays the content within the tags only when viewed from a mobile phone on *http://m.facebook.com*. Does not appear to work on Apple iPhones.

FBML-Specific Attributes

Required

None.

Optional

None.

Example FBML

Here is example FBML code for the `<fb:mobile/>` tag. All content outside the `<fb:mobile/>` block will not be rendered on mobile phones:

```
This text will not appear on the mobile phone.
<fb:mobile>
This text will appear on the mobile phone.
</fb:mobile>
```

<fb:google-analytics/>

`<fb:google-analytics uacct="..." ... >...</fb:google-analytics>`

Renders the standard Google Analytics JavaScript code in the place where you put the tags. For more information on Google Analytics, refer to *http://analytics.google.com* and *http://www.google.com/urchin/index.html*. Basically, Google Analytics and Google's Urchin Software analyze your site traffic and provide you with reports about how your visitors use your site.

FBML-Specific Attributes

Required

`uacct=[`*`string`*`] default: none`
: The Urchin or Google account ID provided to you by Google Analytics. It's often the text in the variable `_uacct` provided in the JavaScript that Google gives you.

Optional

Based on *http://wiki.developers.facebook.com/index.php/Fb:google-analytics*, the following optional attributes are available:

`page=[`*`string`*`] default: none`
: The argument given to the `urchinTracker( )` function; either a page or a virtual page.

`ufsc=[1|0] default: 1`
: Sets the client info flag, where `1` = on and `0` = off. This is an Urchin Traffic Monitor (UTM) user setting.

`udn=[auto|none|domain] default: auto`
: Sets the domain name for cookies. Specify `auto`, `none`, or `domain`. This is a UTM user setting.

`uhash=[on|off] default: on`
: Specify whether the unique domain hash for cookies is `on` or `off`. This is a UTM user setting.

utimeout=[*int*] default: 1800
: Sets the inactive session timeout in seconds. This is a UTM user setting.

ugifpath=[*string*] default: /__utm.gif
: Sets the web path to the *__utm.gif* file. This is a UTM user setting.

utsp=[*string*] default: |
: Sets the transaction field separator. This is a UTM user setting.

uflash=[1|0] default: 1
: Sets the Flash version detection option, where `1` = on and `0` = off. This is a UTM user setting.

utitle=[1|0] default: 1
: Sets the document title detection option, where `1` = on and `0` = off. This is a UTM user setting.

ulink=[1|0] default: 0
: Enables linker functionality, where `1` = on and `0` = off. This is a UTM user setting.

uanchor=[1|0] default: 0
: Indicates whether the use of anchors for campaigns is enabled, where `1` = enabled and `0` = disabled. This is a UTM user setting.

utcp=[*string*] default: /
: Specifies the cookie path for tracking. This is a UTM user setting.

usample=[1...100] default: 100
: Represents the sampling percentage of visitors to track, which is a whole number from 1 to 100. This is a UTM user setting.

uctm=[1|0] default: 1
: Sets the campaign tracking module state, where `1` = off and `0` = on. This is a UTM campaign tracking setting.

ucto=[*int*] default: 15768000
: Sets the timeout in seconds. This is a UTM campaign tracking setting.

uccn=[*string*] default: utm_campaign
: The name of the campaign. This is a UTM campaign tracking setting.

ucmd=[cpc|cpm|link|email|organic] default: utm_medium
: Represents the campaign medium. Specify `cpc`, `cpm`, `link`, `email`, or `organic`. This is a UTM campaign tracking setting.

ucsr=[*string*] default: utm_source
: Represents the campaign source. This is a UTM campaign tracking setting.

uctr=[*string*] default: utm_term
: The campaign term or keyword. This is a UTM campaign tracking setting.

ucct=[*string*] default: utm_content
: Represents the campaign content. This is a UTM campaign tracking setting.

ucid=[*int*] default: utm_id
: Represents the campaign ID number. This is a UTM campaign tracking setting.

ucno=[*string*] default: utm_nooverride
: Indicates whether or not to override the campaign. This is a UTM campaign tracking setting.

Example FBML

Implementing `<fb:google-analytics/>` is actually quite simple. First, go to *http://analytics.google.com* and set up an account and a new site to track. When it asks you to verify the code on the site, you can ignore that part. Take the `_uacct` number from the JavaScript you were provided and plug it into your Facebook application. The FBML code will look something like this:

```
<fb:google-analytics uacct="UA-1279896-6" page="" />
```

Rendered HTML for Single Instance of Tag

The example yields HTML that looks something like this:

```
<script src="http://www.google-analytics.com/urchin.js"
    type="text/javascript">
</script>
<script type="text/javascript">
        _uacct = "UA-1279896-6";
        urchinTracker();
</script>
```

Additional Information

- If you want to do any link tracing, you can utilize FBJS on any links to access your Urchin Tracker through the `Facebook.urchinTracker()` method. Simply write something like the following code (taken from *http://wiki.developers.facebook.com/index.php/Fb:google-analytics*):

  ```
  <a href="http://www.example.com" onclick="Facebook.urchinTracker
      ('/outgoing/example.com')">
  ```

- This tag will work only on canvas pages. Profile pages will render nothing. It is unclear at the time of this writing how this tag will work in the new design on pages other than canvas pages.

<fb:18-plus/>

`<fb:18-plus>...</fb:18-plus>`

Renders the enclosed content only if the viewing user is 18-years-old or older. Supports `<fb:else/>` tags. It is believed that this tag was developed in order to satisfy laws for alcohol-related Facebook apps. Facebook has a global audience, and in many places around the world, alcohol is legal for those who are 18 and older, whereas other places allow it only for those who are 21 and older.

FBML-Specific Attributes

Required

None.

Optional

None.

Example FBML

Here is example FBML code for the `<fb:18-plus/>` tag. Only the text within the tags will appear to those 18 and older:

```
<fb:18-plus>
  This will be displayed to 18 and older people.
  <fb:else>All 17 and younger will see this.</fb:else>
</fb:18-plus>
```

<fb:21-plus/>

`<fb:21-plus>...</fb:21-plus>`

Renders the enclosed content only if the viewing user is 21-years-old or older. Supports `<fb:else/>` tags. As with the **`<fb:18-plus>`** tag, it is believed that this tag was developed in order to satisfy laws for alcohol-related Facebook apps. Facebook has a global audience, and in many places around the world, alcohol is legal for those who are 18 and older, whereas other places allow it only for those who are 21 and older.

FBML-Specific Attributes

Required

None.

Optional

None.

Example FBML

Here is example FBML code for the <fb:21-plus/> tag. Only the text within the tags will appear to those 21 and older:

```
<fb:21-plus>
  This will be displayed to 21 and older people.
  <fb:else>All 20 and younger will see this.</fb:else>
</fb:21-plus>
```

<fb:is-it-christmas/>

<fb:is-it-christmas>...</fb:is-it-christmas>

Renders the enclosed content only if it's Christmas day. Something of an Easter egg feature, this tag was released for fun around Christmas 2007. It is unclear how long it will be supported.

FBML-Specific Attributes

Required

None.

Optional

None.

Example FBML

Here is example FBML code for the <fb:is-it-christmas/> tag:

```
<fb:is-it-christmas>
  Ho! Ho! Ho!
<fb:else>
  Have a good day!
</fb:else>
</fb:is-it-christmas>
```

Additional Information

- Supports the <fb:else/> tag.

<fb:is-it-april-fools/>

<fb:is-it-april-fools>...</fb:is-it-april-fools>

This is no April fools joke! Facebook actually has an FBML tag that renders the content enclosed within the tags only if it's April Fools' Day. This can be a great way to have some fun with your users on April Fools' Day. Something of an Easter egg feature, this tag was released for fun around April 1, 2008. It is unclear how long it will be supported.

FBML-Specific Attributes

Required

None.

Optional

None.

Example FBML

Here is example FBML code for the `<fb:is-it-april-fools/>` tag:

```
<fb:is-it-april-fools>
  April Fools!
<fb:else>
  Have a good day!
</fb:else>
</fb:is-it-april-fools>
```

Additional Information

- Supports the `<fb:else/>` tag.

<fb:rock-the-vote/>

`<fb:rock-the-vote ... >...</fb:rock-the-vote>`

This tag is interesting because it's the first FBML tag sponsored by a third party. The year 2008—when this book is being released—is a Presidential campaign and election year, and Facebook decided to offer developers a way to help their users register to vote. So Facebook partnered with Rock the Vote and CREDO Mobile to provide this service though a simple Facebook tag. The tag displays a link on your app that, when clicked, pops up a voter registration form. You can optionally provide a Rock the Vote API key given to you at *http://www.rockthevote.com/partners*, which allows you to track the number of voter registrations your app has enabled.

FBML-Specific Attributes

Required

None.

Optional

`api_key=[`*`the API key supplied to you at http://www.rockthevote.com/partners`*`] default: none`

The API key provided by *http://www.rockthevote.com/partners* that allows you to track the number of voter registrations made through your app.

Example FBML

To place a Rock the Vote link in your app, just enter FBML code like this:

```
<fb:rock-the-vote>
  Not registered to vote yet? Click here!
</fb:rock-the-vote>
```

Rendered HTML for Single Instance of Tag

The example produces a link that looks like Figure 3-53.

Not registered to vote yet? Click here!

Figure 3-53. Rock the Vote link on your app

When you click on the link, a form that looks like Figure 3-54 will pop up as a dialog box.

Additional Information

- Again, to track registrations, you can obtain an API key at *http://www.rockthevote.com/partners*.

Dynamic FBML Attributes

From within your FBML, you can apply special attributes to specific FBML and HTML tags that allow you to perform AJAX, dynamically hide and show elements, and other common JavaScript functions. The methods in this section offer you an easy way to get things done without having to worry too much about getting JavaScript to work in Facebook.

Visibility Attributes

With just a few attributes added to most elements in your FBML, you can dynamically allow the displaying and hiding of data upon a click of a mouse button. The following attributes can include more than one element ID, separated by commas:

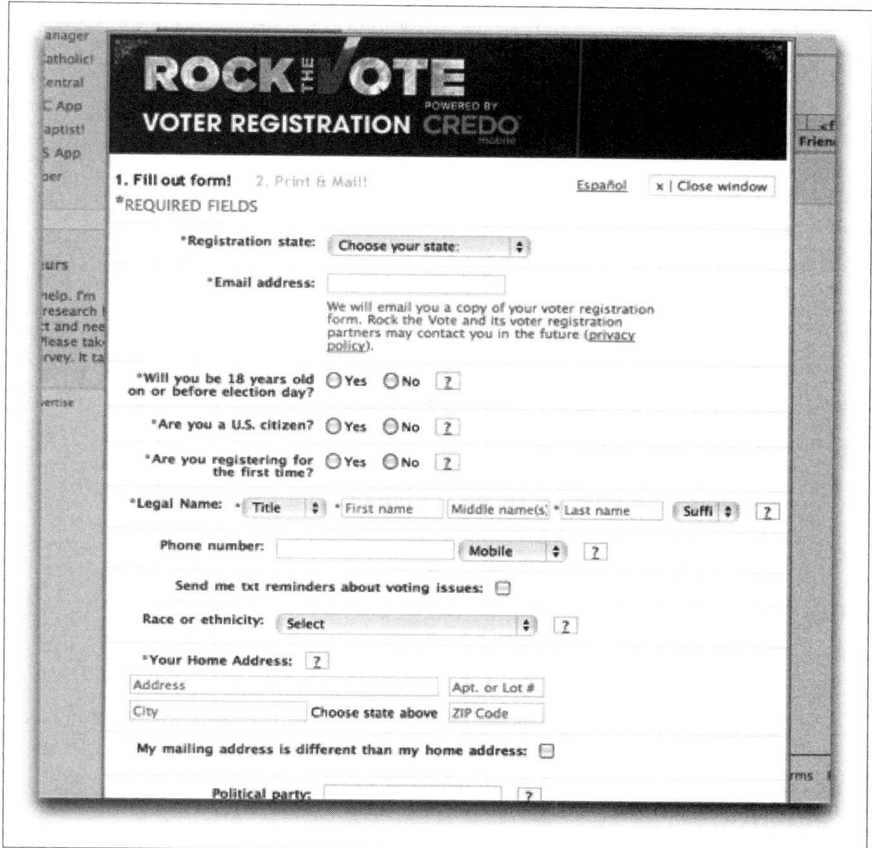

Figure 3-54. Rock the Vote pop-up form

`clicktoshow`
: When the current element is clicked, the element IDs contained will switch to `display:block`.

`clicktohide`
: When the current element is clicked, the element IDs contained will switch to `display:none`.

`clicktotoggle`
: When the current element is clicked, the element IDs contained will switch between their existing state and `display:none` and vice versa, depending on the current state.

`clickthrough`
: Set this to `true` when using radio buttons or checkboxes with which you want to use `clicktoshow`, `clicktohide`, or `clicktotoggle`. Not setting

clickthrough="true" when using these elements will render the element inoperable.

Here are three examples that show how to use the visibility attributes:

```
<div id="example1" style="display:none">Visible</div>
<a href="#" clicktoshow="example1">Click here to make "Visible"
    appear.</a>

<div id="example2">Visible2</div>
<a href="#" clicktohide="example2">Click here to make "Visible2"
    dissapear.</a>

<div id="example3">Visible3</div>
<a href="#" clicktotoggle="example1,example2,example3">
  Click here to toggle visibility of Visible1, Visible2, and Visible3
</a>
```

It is important to note that all styling (display:none, display:block, etc.) that is affected by the attributes just described should be done inline, via style attributes. Styling cannot be done inside a stylesheet document or via <style/> tags.

Mock AJAX

Mock AJAX is a tool that, through simple attributes added to elements of HTML and FBML, allows dynamic loading of data via AJAX directly from your own servers. If you add a few attributes to a simple submit button, upon a click of that submit button, the specified element will refresh with the specified content from your servers. Here are the attributes available:

clickrewriteid
: The ID of the element on the page to be refreshed.

clickrewriteurl
: The URL on your servers (this cannot be a Facebook URL!) that returns data to be refreshed into the specified element.

clickrewriteform
: The form that will be submitted upon a click of the button containing these attributes.

Mock AJAX works on anything that can be clicked, but it must submit a form on the page when clicked. Here's some example code using Mock AJAX:

```
<form id="ajax_form">
  <input type="text" name="test"/>
</form>
<a href="#" clickrewriteid="data" clickrewriteurl=
    "http://fbmlessentials.staynalive.com/mockajax.php"
  clickrewriteform="ajax_form">Click here to load the data</a>
<div id="data"></div>
```

To test the return data, inspect the term `FBML.mockAjaxResponse` using a development tool such as Firefox's Firebug. The data within should give you clues as to what is going on. I strongly recommend using Firebug to debug your Mock AJAX calls.

Data Access for JavaScript and Dynamic Rendering in FBML

<fb:js-string/>

`<fb:js-string var="...">...</fb:js-string>`

Loads rendered FBML into a JavaScript variable to be accessed later via FBJS. This can be a great way to render FBML before passing it to the JavaScript.

FBML-Specific Attributes

Required

`var=[string] default: none`
The name of the variable that can be accessed later via FBJS.

Optional

None.

Example FBML

Here is example FBML code for the `<fb:js-string/>` tag:

```
<fb:js-string var="test_var">
  Hello <fb:name uid="loggedinuser"/>!
</fb:js-string>
<div id="test_div"></div>
<a href="#" onclick="document.getElementById('test_div').
    setInnerFBML(test_var)">Display test_div</a>
```

<fb:fbml/>

`<fb:fbml>...</fb:fbml>`

Renders a block within a particular version of FBML. This is especially useful when testing a beta version of a tag, or if you want to ensure your FBML will always work as Facebook makes upgrades to FBML.

FBML-Specific Attributes

Required

None.

Optional

`version=[float] default: the current version`
: The version of FBML to parse the enclosed content under.

Example FBML

Here is example FBML code for the `<fb:fbml/>` tag:

```
<fb:fbml version="1.0">
This content would be parsed under FBML version 1.0 instead of the
    current version (1.1).
</fb:fbml>
```

<fb:ref/>

`<fb:ref [url="..."|handle="..."]/>`

Allows the developer to reference FBML, whether it be from Facebook's servers or an external URL. When `handle` is used, Facebook references a cached handle stored on the Facebook servers that is set via the `fbml.setRefHandle` API method. When `url` is used, Facebook references FBML retrieved from a URL that you specify that it has cached on its servers. With `url`, you have to use the `fbml.refreshRefUrl` API method.

FBML-Specific Attributes

Required

`url=[string] default: none`
: The URL of the content to be loaded. Whenever this tag is called with that URL, the content originally cached on Facebook's servers will be loaded in place. This is a great way to dynamically load content onto a user's profile. You must specify either `url` or `ref`, but not both.

`ref=[string] default: none`
: The `ref` handle that points to data that was previously stored via the API method call, `fbml.setRefHandle`. Whenever this tag is called for that `ref` handle, that content will be loaded. This keeps you from having to continuously load data from your servers. It is also an excellent way to dynamically load content into a user's profile. You must specify either `url` or `ref`, but not both.

Optional

None.

Example FBML

Two examples follow. Imagine these placed on a user's profile. (They work on the canvas page as well.)

First, assuming you made the API call:

```
fbml.setRefHandle("test_handle","Hello <fb:name uid='loggedinuser'/>");
```

then, anywhere you load:

```
<fb:ref ref="test_handle"/>
```

will display:

```
Hello <fb:name uid='loggedinuser'/>
```

Alternatively, if *http://fbmlessentials.staynalive.com/ref.php* were to contain:

```
Example url usage of &lt;fb:ref/&gt;
```

then, if you called the following on a canvas or profile page:

```
<fb:ref url="http://fbmlessentials.staynalive.com/ref.php"/>
```

this tag would be rendered as the following HTML:

```
Example url usage of &lt;fb:ref/&gt;
```

Additional Information

- Nested `<fb:ref/>`s are allowed.

Now that you've made it this far, let's spend some time learning a little about FBJS, Facebook's own set of JavaScript libraries, in Chapter 4.

CHAPTER 4

FBJS Reference

Introduction

JavaScript is very possible to use in Facebook applications. A book about FBML would not be complete without at least a short introduction to FBJS. I'm going to keep this discussion "in a nutshell," but you can find much more information on the Facebook Developer Wiki at *http://wiki.developers.facebook.com/index.php/FBJS*.

FBJS is a very limited form of JavaScript, which Facebook has placed controls on to prevent malicious code in applications from accessing data it shouldn't. Privacy is of the utmost importance on Facebook, and FBJS controls reflect that. Despite the restrictions, with a little practice, FBJS can provide almost all necessary functions that JavaScript can provide in an external application.

For even more flexibility in a JavaScript-heavy site, you should take some time and look up the JavaScript Client Library on the Facebook Developer Wiki: *http://wiki.developers.facebook.com/index.php/JavaScript_Client_Library*.

General Information

JavaScript in Facebook, just like FBML and HTML, gets parsed and rewritten by Facebook before it is rendered for the user. Therefore, it is important that you follow some specific rules to ensure that your JavaScript is fully compatible with Facebook. The rules to keep in mind are as follows:

- JavaScript methods and variables should be prepended with the application ID, followed by an "_" in Facebook. This won't affect your code too much, but it's important to remember, as in certain instances you may need to call the method or variable with the application ID attached. In most cases you can just call the method name or variable name by itself and Facebook will handle all the magic!

- On profiles, JavaScript will not run without the user making some sort of click action first. Therefore, it's necessary to have an `onClick` event handler of some sort within a link or element in order to launch anything on profile pages. On canvas pages, the click action is not necessary.
- Most DOM methods will work, but to retrieve information you must prepend the method with `get`. To set information, you must prepend the method name with `set`, and rather than assigning a value via the = sign, you must instead pass in the value as a variable. So, instead of:

  ```
  document.getElementById('my_div').innerHTML = 'test content';
  ```

  you would do this in FBJS:

  ```
  document.getElementById('my_div').setInnerHTML('test content');
  ```

  Table 4-1 lists all the methods available and their `get` and `set` equivalents (this list is taken from the Developer Wiki).

The JavaScript methods in this table that have no descriptions work the same way they do in normal JavaScript.

Table 4-1. FBJS methods

JavaScript method	FBJS "get" equivalent	FBJS "set" equivalent	Description
`parentNode`	`getParentNode`		
`nextSibling`	`getNextSibling`		
`previousSibling`	`getPreviousSibling`		
`firstChild`	`getFirstChild`		
`lastChild`	`getLastChild`		
`childNodes`	`getChildNodes`		
`innerHTML`		`setInnerFBML`	Direct strings passed to this method may throw an error. Pass all strings to `<fb:js-string/>` first, and then load the variable from that. Note that you cannot do `getInnerHTML`.
`innerHTML`		`setInnerXHTML`	XHTML/HTML passed to this method gets sanitized by Facebook. Note that you cannot do `getInnerHTML`.

JavaScript method	FBJS "get" equivalent	FBJS "set" equivalent	Description
innerText/textContent		setTextValue	Allows plain-text values only; child nodes get removed. There is no get equivalent.
form			Use document.getElementById('form_id') instead.
action	getAction	setAction	
value	getValue	setValue	
href	getHref	setHref	
target	getTarget	setTarget	
src	getSrc	setSrc	
className	getClassName	setClassName	
		addClassName(className)	Adds className as a new class.
		removeClassName(className)	Removes the class className.
		toggleClassName(className)	If the class className exists, removes it. If not, adds it.
		hasClassName(className)	Returns true if className exists. Returns false otherwise.
tagName	getTagName		
id	getId	setId	
dir	getDir	setDir	
checked	getChecked	setChecked	
clientWidth	getClientWidth		
clientHeight	getClientHeight		
offsetWidth	getOffsetWidth		
offsetHeight	getOffsetHeight		
	getAbsoluteTop		Returns the absolute position from the top of the page.
	getAbsoluteLeft		Returns the absolute position from the left of the page.
scrollTop	getScrollTop	setScrollTop	
scrollLeft	getScrollLeft	setScrollLeft	

JavaScript method	FBJS "get" equivalent	FBJS "set" equivalent	Description
scrollHeight	getScrollHeight		
scrollWidth	getScrollWidth		
tabIndex	getTabIndex	setTabIndex	
title	getTitle	setTitle	
name	getName	setName	
cols	getCols	setCols	
rows	getRows	setRows	
accessKey	getAccessKey	setAccessKey	
disabled	getDisabled	setDisabled	
readOnly	getReadOnly	setReadOnly	
type	getType	setType	
selectedIndex	getSelectedIndex	setSelectedIndex	
selected	getSelected	setSelected	
location		setLocation	
style	getStyle	setStyle	
	getRootElement		Returns the topmost element of your profile box or canvas page.
	getSelection	setSelection(start, end)	Allows the retrieval and setting of values in a text-box element.

One of the biggest headaches in FBJS is the lack of `get` methods for `innerHTML`-type methods. You can get around this by setting a variable and manipulating that, and then accessing that variable in your JavaScript.

Event Listeners

`addEventListener` and `removeEventListener` work just as they do in regular JavaScript. However, `addEventListener` in FBJS does not support the `useCapture` parameter. In addition, Facebook provides the following methods:

`listEventListeners(eventName)`
: Returns an array of identifiers for all events that have been added to this event.

`purgeEventListeners(eventName)`
: Removes all event listeners for the specified event.

AJAX

Facebook provides an AJAX class that developers can access to implement simple AJAX calls. The AJAX class supports the following properties:

`ondone(data)`
: An event handler that is called when the AJAX call is returned. `data` can be an object, string, or FBML string.

`onerror`
: An event handler that is called when an error is generated by the AJAX call.

`requireLogin`
: If set to `true`, forces the user to be logged in before an AJAX call can be made to the application owner's server. Once logged in, it will pass the `fb_sig` values back to your server as part of the call.

In addition to those properties, the AJAX class supports the following methods:

`post(url,query)`
: Starts an AJAX post to the given URL with the given query parameters.

`abort()`
: Aborts the AJAX post.

Here is some sample AJAX code that mimics the Mock AJAX examples we used in Chapter 3. I like to include this in all of my Facebook applications, since it provides slightly more flexibility than a simple Mock AJAX call:

```
<script>
function do_ajax(url, div_id) {
  var ajax = new Ajax();
  ajax.responseType = Ajax.FBML;
  ajax.ondone = function(data) {
    document.getElementById(div_id).setInnerFBML(data);
  }
  ajax.requireLogin = true;
  ajax.post(url);
}
</script>
```

In this example I instantiate a new AJAX object, and set its response type as FBML, since I know my servers will always return FBML. When the request is done, I assign `ondone()` an anonymous callback function that sets the inside of the given `div` ID with the returned data. I require the user to be logged in, and finally, I make an AJAX post to the given URL. You could call this function with the following HTML:

```
<div id="my_div">Please Wait...</div>
<a href="#" onclick="do_ajax
```

```
    ('http://fbmlessentials.staynalive.com/ajax.php','my_div')">
  Click here to load the div
</a>
```

When the user clicks the "Click here to load the div" link, the text that says "Please Wait..." will quickly turn to the contents returned by the HTML that the URL passed into `do_ajax` renders.

Dialogs

Besides the `<fb:dialog/>` FBML tag, you can also use FBJS to render dialogs. FBJS dialogs give you slightly added flexibility that you don't get from FBML. The way to initiate a dialog box is simply by instantiating a new `Dialog` object via the DOM. The following are the methods supported by the `Dialog` class:

`Dialog(type)`
: The constructor for `Dialog`. Note that `type` can be one of either `Dialog.DIALOG_POP` or `Dialog.DIALOG_CONTEXTUAL`:

  `Dialog.DIALOG_POP`
  : Renders a dialog box that looks like Figure 4-1.

  `Dialog.DIALOG_CONTEXTUAL`
  : Renders a dialog box that looks like Figure 4-2.

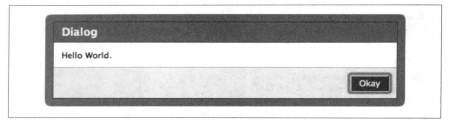

Figure 4-1. DIALOG_POP

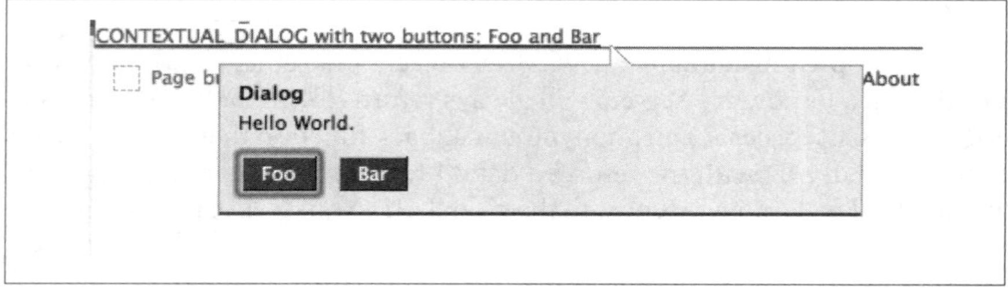

Figure 4-2. DIALOG_CONTEXTUAL

`onconfirm`
: Event handler that gets triggered when the leftmost button is clicked in the dialog.

`oncancel`
: Event handler that gets triggered when the rightmost button is clicked in the dialog.

`setStyle`
: Sets the style of the parent dialog box.

`showMessage(title, content, button_confirm = 'Okay')`
: Renders a dialog box with just one confirm button, similar to an "alert" box. The title and content can be either pure text or FBML content using a variable from something like `<fb:js-string/>`.

`showChoice(title, content, button_confirm = 'Okay', button_cancel = 'Cancel')`
: Renders a dialog box with both a confirm and a cancel button. The title and content can be either pure text or FBML content using a variable from something like `<fb:js-string/>` .

`setContext`
: Useful only with `DIALOG_CONTEXTUAL`; sets where the pointer of the bubble should point (see Figure 4-2).

`hide`
: Hides the dialog box.

You can initiate a dialog box using something like the following FBML code (this example is taken from the Developer Wiki):

```
<a href="#" onclick="new Dialog().showMessage
    ('Dialog', 'Hello World.'); return false;">
DIALOG_POP.</a><br />
```

Alternatively, you could use:

```
<a href="#" onclick="new Dialog
    (Dialog.DIALOG_CONTEXTUAL).setContext(this).showChoice
    ('Dialog', 'Hello World.', 'Foo', 'Bar'); return false;">
CONTEXTUAL_DIALOG with two buttons: Foo and Bar</a><br />
```

The first example renders a `DIALOG_POPUP` when you click on it, similar to the screenshot in Figure 4-1. The second example renders a `DIALOG_CONTEXTUAL` when you click on it, similar to the screenshot in Figure 4-2.

Visualization

Facebook also provides a fairly rich JavaScript Animations library. With this library you can "tween" (an animation term, short for "in-betweening") CSS attributes, and hide, fade, and make elements appear, among other things. Although this is out of the scope of this book, you can learn more on the Facebook Developer Wiki at *http://wiki.developers.facebook.com/index.php/FBJS/Animation*.

Conclusion

As you've seen, Facebook offers a very rich platform for which developers can build applications. With FBML, Facebook provides many tools and shortcuts for developers to accelerate their work on these applications even further. Facebook continues to add more features and tags (three or four tags were added in the last month of this writing!). It is definitely a development platform worth considering.

It is my hope that as you've read this book, or even just used it as a reference, you've gained something from the materials provided. I believe Facebook is here to stay. It is worth having a part in as it takes off like a windstorm! So grab on, and enjoy the ride.

Afterword

Now that you have read *FBML Essentials*, you have the tools you need from a coding perspective. I think that this book will become your bible for getting your code together to make your Facebook app perform exactly as you desire.

It is important that you take what you have learned from this book and apply it to your work in creative, unique, and compelling ways that will engage the users of your shiny new Facebook application. Find a way to leverage the social graph and bring interesting connections to the surface. Facebook gives you this opportunity; it is in your best interest to think hard on this point.

I would encourage you to look at other applications that have high engagement rates and high levels of daily active users and see what you can learn from what they have implemented. Think about what makes a compelling application. Do not try to shoehorn an existing website into Facebook in a way that results in a depreciated user experience. That type of application will almost always fail on Facebook.

I have looked at and evaluated well over 4,000 applications on the Facebook Platform. I have learned that what makes an application successful on Facebook is its ability to provide self-expression, personal and microtouch connections, and a way to do something unique and different. Always be looking for ways to allow your application to spread virally based on user interaction with its core functionality.

Take a strategic look at what you want your application to achieve. What are your business, marketing, and user engagement objectives? Fortune 500 companies may benefit from an application that is strategically designed for optimal goal attainment. Small businesses and startups can also reach the 70+ million users on Facebook with a properly executed application.

I would also tell you to measure your app's performance with some third-party analytics. You will want to make iterations and do some A/B testing, if possible. Measure, iterate, measure, iterate. Repeat as required.

Always look at your application through the eyes of your users. They will tell you what they do and don't like on your app's About page. Make sure you listen to them and respond quickly to their concerns.

As I like to say, "The only constant on Facebook is change." Leverage the changes that come your way, and embrace them as potential opportunities to do new things that your application users will like.

Jesse has given you the direction to properly use FBML with this great book. Use it often and it will save you hours of frustration.

My parting words here are to encourage you to have a well-constructed strategy before you charge down the road and throw an app onto Facebook without first thinking through what you want to attain. Know where you want to go and how you are going to get there by giving users what they want. If you don't know how to do this, find the people who can help you through this ideation and strategy process. Welcome to the brave and quickly evolving world of the Facebook application. Now go out there and create, and dare to be great!

Cheers!

—Rodney Rumford
CEO: *http://www.GravitationalMedia.com*
Editor: *http://www.facereviews.com*

Index

We'd like to hear your suggestions for improving our indexes. Send email to *index@oreilly.com*.

C

D

E

F

G

H

I

J

Q

R

S

T

U

V

W

X

About the Author

Jesse Stay runs his own social media consulting and development business, and has consulted for some of the top 100 applications on Facebook. Within just two months, he successfully sold his first Facebook application, which he wrote in just one week. He is the author of *I'm On Facebook—Now What???* (Happy About), a book targeted toward helping individuals and business owners better manage their lives through Facebook. You can follow him on his blog, *http://www.staynalive.com*.

Colophon

The animal on the cover of *FBML Essentials* is a white-throated dipper (*Cinclus cinclus*), an aquatic songbird found throughout Europe, the UK, and the Middle East. It is especially common in Britain and Ireland. Around seven inches long, the dipper is round, squat, and short-tailed. Adult white-throated dippers have dark plumage and a prominent white breast, with a reddish band above a black belly. Young dippers are gray and lack the reddish band.

Dippers live near fast-flowing streams and rivers, and they swim underwater to hunt for small fish and shrimps. Some people believe that the bird walks along the bottom of a river, using its wings and strong feet to keep itself submerged, but by most accounts the dipper swims, using its wings to "fly" underwater. Like other waterfowl, the dipper has a translucent eyelid called a nictitating membrane that protects its eye when it dives. Oils produced from a gland above its tail keep the dipper warm and make its feathers nearly waterproof.

The dipper's nest is made from straw and moss, about the size and shape of a soccer ball. This nest is usually built into the hollow of a rock, in a crevice under a bridge or stone wall, or on an overhanging branch. When the bird is perched on dry land, it makes a unique bobbing motion by bending and straightening its knees and cocking its tail. The dipper gets its name from this habit of bobbing, not from its water diving. No one knows for certain why the bird dips in this way, but biologists believe the behavior is somehow linked to the dipper's rushing-water environment.

The cover image is from the Dover Pictorial Archive. The cover font is Adobe ITC Garamond. The text font is Linotype Birka; the heading font is Adobe Myriad Condensed; and the code font is LucasFont's TheSansMonoCondensed.

Related Titles from O'Reilly

Web Authoring and Design

ActionScript 3.0 Cookbook
Ajax Hacks
Ambient Findability
Creating Web Sites: The Missing Manual
CSS Cookbook, *2nd Edition*
CSS Pocket Reference, *2nd Edition*
CSS: The Definitive Guide, *3rd Edition*
CSS: The Missing Manual
Dreamweaver 8: Design and Construction
Dreamweaver 8: The Missing Manual
Dynamic HTML: The Definitive Reference, *3rd Edition*
Essential ActionScript 3.0
Flex 8 Cookbook
Flash 8: Projects for Learning Animation and Interactivity
Flash 8: The Missing manual
Flash 9 Design: Motion Graphics for Animation & User Interfaces
Flash Hacks
Head First HTML with CSS & XHTML
Head Rush Ajax
Head First Web Design
High Performance Web Sites
HTML & XHTML: The Definitive Guide, *6th Edition*
HTML & XHTML Pocket Reference, *3rd Edition*
Information Architecture for the World Wide Web, *3rd Edition*
Information Dashboard Design
JavaScript: The Definitive Guide, *5th Edition*
JavaScript & DHTML Cookbook, *2nd Edition*
Learning ActionScript 3.0
Learning JavaScript
Learning Web Design, *3rd Edition*
PHP Hacks
Programming Collective Intelligence
Programming Flex 2
Web Design in a Nutshell, *3rd Edition*
Web Site Measurement Hacks

Our books are available at most retail and online bookstores.
To order direct: 1-800-998-9938 • *order@oreilly.com* • *www.oreilly.com*
Online editions of most O'Reilly titles are available by subscription at *safari.oreilly.com*

The O'Reilly Advantage

Stay Current and Save Money

Order books online:
www.oreilly.com/store/order

Questions about our products or your order:
order@oreilly.com

Join our email lists: Sign up to get topic specific email announcements or new books, conferences, special offers and technology news
elists.oreilly.com

For book content technical questions:
booktech@oreilly.com

To submit new book proposals to our editors:
proposals@oreilly.com

Contact us:
O'Reilly Media, Inc.
1005 Gravenstein Highway N.
Sebastopol, CA U.S.A. 95472
707-827-7000 or
800-998-9938
www.oreilly.com

Did you know that if you register your O'Reilly books, you'll get automatic notification and upgrade discounts on new editions?

And that's not all! Once you've registered your books you can:

» Win free books, T-shirts and O'Reilly Gear

» Get special offers available only to registered O'Reilly customers

» Get free catalogs announcing all our new titles (US and UK Only)

Registering is easy! Just go to www.oreilly.com/go/register

Try the online edition free for 45 days

Get the information you need when you need it, with Safari Books Online. Safari Books Online contains the complete version of the print book in your hands plus thousands of titles from the best technical publishers, with sample code ready to cut and paste into your applications.

Safari is designed for people in a hurry to get the answers they need so they can get the job done. You can find what you need in the morning, and put it to work in the afternoon. As simple as cut, paste, and program.

To try out Safari and the online edition of the above title FREE for 45 days, go to www.oreilly.com/go/safarienabled and enter the coupon code MKAIGCB.

To see the complete Safari Library visit:
safari.oreilly.com

70502